THE MIND OF PIUS XII

THE MIND OF

PIUS XII

EDITED BY

Robert C. Pollock

Associate Professor of History and Philosophy,
Graduate School, Fordham University

CROWN PUBLISHERS, INC. ⸱ NEW YORK

For permission to quote I gratefully acknowledge the courtesy of the following publishers, periodicals and individuals: The Rev. Robert C. Hartnett, S.J., editor of America (America Press Publications: The Catholic Mind *and the pamphlets* Pope Pius XII on the World Community *and* The Church and Modern Science); *the Rev. James A. Magner* (The American Ecclesiastical Review); *The Bruce Publishing Company* (Canon Law Digest, *by Timothy L. Bouscaren, S.J.); Catholic Canon Law Society, The Catholic University of America* (Seminar); *Pontifical Court Club, Salesian Press, London* (Catholic Documents); *Dodd, Mead & Company* (Angelic Shepherd, *by the Most Rev. Jan Olav Smit) and its translator the Rev. James H. Vanderveldt, O.F.M., of The Catholic University of America; Harcourt, Brace & Company* (The Pope Speaks, *by Charles Rankin); the Rev. P. J. Hamell, D.D., editor, St. Patrick's College, Maynooth, Ireland* (Irish Ecclesiastical Record); *Irish Monthly, Dublin; Mr. Henry P. Lefebure* (National Catholic Welfare Conference Publications: Principles for Peace, *by the Rev. Harry C. Koenig, S.T.D.,* Catholic Action, *the pamphlet* The Moral Limits of Medical Research and Treatment, *and the text used by The Paulist Press in the pamphlet* Women's Duties in Social and Political Life); *Mr. John O'Neil, editor* (The Pope Speaks, The American Quarterly of Papal Documents); *the Rev. John Forest, O.F.M., Director of St. Anthony's Guild, Paterson, N. J.* (National Catholic Almanac); *The Tablet Publishing Company, London* (The Tablet); *the Rev. Vincent A. Yzermans* (The Unwearied Advocate). *I also thank The Paulist Press for the use I made of their pamphlets of Papal Encyclicals.*

REGINAE OMNIUM MARIAE

"... the Church has affirmed the value of what is human and what is in conformity with nature. ..."

—Pius XII

"... There is no opposition between the laws that govern the life of faithful Christians and the postulates of a genuine humane humanitarianism, but rather unity and mutual support. ..."

—Pius XII

Contents

Errata

Page 102, second line from bottom, "original" should read "origin."
Page 111, *The meeting of spirit and Spirit,* third line, "spirit"
should read "Spirit."

ACKNOWLEDGMENTS

I wish to express my deep gratitude to the Rev. Thurston N. Davis, S.J., an associate editor of *America*, for his generous assistance. I am also indebted to the Rev. Vincent A. Yzermans of St. Cloud, Minnesota, for his friendly interest, and to Mother Ruth Dowd, R.S.C.J., of Manhattanville College of the Sacred Heart, for her cooperation in gathering a number of texts. To Miss Margaret Halligan, M.A., of New York City, I owe a special debt of gratitude for her painstaking research and her wholehearted sympathy with the project. I also wish to thank Mr. Edward F. Murphy, of New York City, for his friendly support and his research labors. I am happy to acknowledge here the personal and valuable cooperation of Mr. Millen Brand of the staff of Crown Publishers, as well as the personal interest shown by other members of the staff. Throughout, my wife Jean's assistance was indispensable—in research, in helping to give the book its structure, and in disposing efficiently of endless details.

R.C.P.

Marlow, N. H.

Foreword

IN READING through the communications of His Holiness, Pope Pius XII, one is struck by a breadth of view which catches in its embrace the totality of human life. Whatever properly belongs in the human scheme is regarded with reverence, and its value appraised against the background of modern knowledge and experience. Religion, as we see the pattern unfold in these communications, offers us "a vision of the whole, of the present as of the future, of matter as of spirit, of time as of eternity," a vision in which we can truly apprehend the magnificence of man, and not merely his wretchedness.

It is just such a vision which has enlarged and deepened the humanistic spirit inherited from Classical civilization, and whose finest expression is found in Catholic traditions of thought. The Pope, therefore, speaks with the power of doctrine and history when he points out that all that humanism "contains of the true, the good, the great and the eternal belongs to the spiritual world of the greatest genius of the Middle Ages, St. Thomas Aquinas."

Since the beginning of his Pontificate, Pius XII has accomplished noteworthy things, but there is one achievement in particular whose significance very few today will fail to grasp, once it is made known to them. In describing this achievement we would say that, essentially, it is a powerful, concrete and sustained presentation of religious life as the true foundation of universality and wholeness. At a time when men are seeking a conception of things which will bring universality of vision and fullness of life to a fragmented world, the Pope's achievement is one of the great events of our time. Actually, what he has done is to mobilize the energies of men against an unnatural separation between everyday life and religious life—a separation which for many has become a grim reality.

Looking at the world, His Holiness perceives this cleavage and its awful consequences, but he bids us take heart, in showing us that if man has dug a chasm between his earthly interests and religion, God easily spans it with His omnipotence and love. Thus the Pontiff reminds us that "the spirit of Christ still breathes gently on His world." And to those who have forgotten the divine presence, he holds aloft the luminous truth, that the Divine Spirit, while distinct from the world, is not outside it, "nor secluded as it were in disdainful isolation," while abandoning to itself a world created by Him out of superabundant love. Moreover, he points to the sublime truth that nothing escapes God's providence, and that there is nothing great nor small that happens "which is not foreseen, wished or permitted, directed always by providence to its exalted ends."

But the Pope sees more than this, for in the light of integral truth, he does not fail to discern in the world of today elements of human greatness as well as of human littleness. Man is not, in the sight of God, "mere corruption and sin," and "in the eyes of the Church, Original Sin did not intimately affect men's aptitudes and strength, and has left essentially intact the natural light of his intelligence and his freedom." Thus, even though man is "undoubtedly injured and weakened by the heavy inheritance of a fallen nature, deprived of supernatural and preternatural gifts," man's dignity as a free rational being is upheld by the Church, and all that is worthwhile in human life is searched out, affirmed and embraced.

Enlightened by such a noble doctrine of human dignity, we should expect to find that in this, as in every age, even the darkest, there is present in many individuals everywhere a profound aspiration to truth and goodness. And, needless to say, in an age such as ours, the evidence of such aspiration is mountain-high. Moreover, there is much to show that this longing for truth and goodness is so irrepressible that the souls of men are filled with torment before the cheerless abyss between religion and life which has come to be accepted as normal. Hence there is good reason for a renewal of hope, considering also that we have before us the example of the Supreme Pontiff himself, who has responded so adequately to the situation in which many find themselves. We can rejoice, therefore, in doing what so obviously must be done, in answer to the Pope's appeal that we "rekindle in the present generation confidence in God, in itself, and in the future."

It would be difficult to find anything to equal the Pope's celebration of human powers and achievements. One could fill pages with Papal quotations extolling the wonder of man—his daring genius, his spectacular accomplishments, his ceaseless quest for knowledge. Whenever the opportunity presents itself, His Holiness is quick to seize it, so that he may once again remind us of the greatness of man, of man who is "spirit and dust compounded to form the image of the infinite." And, certainly, the opportunity presents itself frequently, since organizations, national and international, representing the widest variety of human interests are forever converging on Rome, and many are addressed (they or groups of delegates) by the Supreme Pastor of Souls.

Even reading through the excerpts contained in this volume we can see how appreciatively the Pope deals with the various kinds of human activity, while uncovering their spiritual values. But, as he shows, the Church is not satisfied merely to acclaim what is good. No, She wishes to go much farther, for not only does She

(xiii)

bless it, but She also endeavors to give it fuller scope within the entire scheme of things as She envisions it. As Pius XII himself says, the "Church takes to herself the fullness of all that is genuinely human wherever and however She finds it, and transforms it into a source of supernatural energy." [1]

The comprehensiveness of the Catholic outlook, as presented by the Holy Father, is breathtaking. To illustrate its sweep, let us take first the universe itself. The universe with its energies waiting to spring forth at man's bidding is glowingly portrayed as the beloved handiwork of God, and as manifesting His presence. Indeed, referring to scientific discoveries, the Pope can exclaim, "Has there ever been a time until now when the presence of God has manifested itself so forcefully—We were about to say, so visibly—to human reason as at the present." Here and in other notable passages in his Addresses he expresses that deep religious emotion before the universe which has been experienced by great Christian souls down the ages.

The authentic Catholic attitude to the universe is such as to delight the heart of those who long for a new fusion of the cosmic sense and the religious sense. As for the Catholic conception of the human body, it should enthrall everyone who wishes to see the material side of man's personal life given its deeper meaning. In this day and age when hygiene, sports and medical triumphs have won the universal spotlight, Pius XII has many opportunities to present the Catholic conception of the human body—the "lofty truths concerning the human body" taught by Revelation and "which confer on the body new value and a more elevated dignity." And in holding before us, not only these truths, but truths taught by right reason and Catholic philosophy, he offers us a doctrine which echoes forth magnificently the Incarnation and its elevation of matter to a new dignity.

To continue, the feats of science are celebrated with eloquence and even with poetic imagination, for the Pope wants us to join

[1] *Catholic Mind*, 44:65. February '46.

him in viewing every scientific discovery as "one more trace of the Divine Intelligence and one more token of the power of God." Furthermore, if he responds with sensitive discernment and depth of feeling to scientific conquests, it is also because, through them, he can make us marvel anew before the splendor of man as the image of a God whose "intellect is infinitely comprehensive."

The wide diffusion of intellectual life among the various classes is viewed as "a marvel in which civilization takes pride." Moreover, he bears witness to the fact that "in many countries large sectors of the population aspire to a participation in an authentic culture." Characteristically, even when he laments moral decadence, even when he castigates spiritual anemia, he does not fail to pay tribute to something positive that has come to the fore in modern life. Thus, he calls attention to "the keen and jealous sense of its own personal dignity and its inner freedom of spirit of which today's conscience boasts." And, in the light of this statement, what he said on one occasion regarding the education of the modern girl can be applied universally: "Was there ever such a time as the present," he exclaims, "when a girl has to be won and trained interiorly, according to her convictions and will, for Christ's cause and a virtuous life. . . ."

Let us pause here for a moment to consider a fact well worth noting, especially now when a negative and pessimistic attitude is so prevalent—that the more we perceive the worthwhile things in our world, the more we are energized to defend them and fight for them. And it is only in and through such a positive approach that we learn to appraise the true proportions of evil. Hence if we learn anything at all from the Pope, it is that the more clearly we perceive the living values within our environment, and delight in them—values which have their ground in God—the more effectively we are challenged by all that would overthrow them. From him, then, we learn that the struggle against evil is also a struggle to save these values—those already established and those struggling forth in pain and difficulty out of the womb of time.

(xv)

To return to our theme—the full scope of the Catholic conception as presented by Pius XII—human personality is portrayed in all its massive grandeur, and by drawing upon the immense resources of Revelation and philosophy. And this grandeur is all the more luminous since human personality is regarded integrally: in relation to God, in terms of real history and concrete society, and within the universe.

The Pontiff's sense of history—that is, of collective humanity in its mysterious journey through time, is bound to have far-reaching effects upon historical consciousness, which, as scholars know, Catholic Christianity was instrumental in developing. With the entire world before him, and in intimate communication with many parts of it, he is delicately sensitive to the universal stirrings within a humanity which is seeking truth and goodness, not through some magical exclusion of time and process, but within their indispensable framework. And he knows that if men are to be brought to a recognition of a transcendent spiritual order, a deeper penetration into the reality of time and process will play its part.

With his sense of history and of humanity, Pius XII is alert to the presence of a ground-swell in the life of mankind today which can have immense moral and spiritual consequences. Thus, he tells us that "To an ever increasing number of noble souls there comes the thought and with it a clearer, stronger determination, to make this universal upheaval a starting point for a new era of far-reaching innovation—the complete reorganization of the world." Again, he notes that, despite the ferment of prejudices and feelings of hate, a consciousness of intimate moral dependence for good or for evil "is more alive and active." And he also points to an awakened faith in "a higher community of man," a real faith, which, as we know is intimately related to the Christian Faith, and, while sustained by it, can also have a quickening effect upon it.

In the light of all that Pius XII says, the true situation of man is borne in on us. We see great multitudes of people in the grip of a terrible restlessness, "a tumult of soul and conscience" which the whirl of material progress cannot still. In fact, conquests in field after field of human endeavor only serve to make the religious problem all the more acute, for instead of appeasing the restless human spirit, they serve to arouse man to an awareness of a mysterious impulse within him which carries him toward the infinite, and, therefore, toward a goal lying beyond the highest peaks of human achievement.

In other words, man is in the grip of a tension—that between his drive to new and greater triumphs and a certain pull toward the infinite which he senses in himself. It is this very tension which accounts for what the Pope refers to as "the spiritual anguish of so many men of good will" and also for the torment of many who have an awareness of spiritual emptiness, which is the first step to spiritual renewal. Here too the Holy Father sums it up for us when he says, "What age has been, for all its technical and purely civic progress, more tormented than ours by spiritual emptiness and deep-felt interior poverty."

Clearly, then, man is in need of a form of religious life which does not drive a wedge between his historical activity and spirituality, but which rather brings them into unity. Men long for that synthesis of life which the Pope portrays as the fruit of the Catholic Faith—a synthesis which would permit them to adhere to God with all their being and yet pursue a wholesome productive life in time and space. Men are ready to respond generously to Christian life lived in its fullness, for they are discovering how dismal and flat a despiritualized way of life can be, and many are groping toward a wholeness which will elevate and revitalize every sphere of human existence and every legitimate activity.

What the Holy Father shows us is that a recognition of the sovereign domain of God over life and destiny does not mean a disparagement of man's works, but rather the recognition of an infinite depth in them. But, above all, he helps us see that we have a choice to make which we cannot evade, that between a sterile restlessness and a fruitful restlessness. And if we choose the latter, we shall experience for ourselves the truth of St. Augustine's words which the Pope has occasion to cite, in discussing depth psychology, "Thou hast made us for Thyself, O Lord, and our heart shall not rest until it rests in Thee."

It is a significant fact that Pius XII holds up the Blessed Contardo Ferrini, modern legal scholar, as a model for the modern Catholic man. And the reason is not far to seek. "Some cannot understand," he tells us, "how a man could live in a world of today, work efficiently and successfully for human society, and at the same time be a saint. . . . Could there possibly exist for the cold and scrutinizing reason of a man of learning, for the mind of a technician who conquers and masters the laws of nature—could there possibly exist a supranatural world and the mysteries of revelation? This question is asked by not a few. Here our Blessed Contardo comes forward and answers with a clear and resolute Yes. . . . He is the man of modern reality, but also the saint of the present hour; *the mystic of the union with God, in Whom he was immersed, and at the same time, so to speak, the mystic of fact and action. . . .*" [1] (italics our own).

How often men are today exhorted to safeguard their common heritage of Christian civilization by many who betray an inadequate comprehension of the full meaning and content of that heritage. Indeed, Pius XII has himself deplored a narrowing of its meaning even on the part of scholars. Yet we have in the large variety of Papal communications a sure guide to the inmost spirit and direction of Christian culture—and in studying these communications we readily see why Christian culture was able to absorb the best in pagan thought and wisdom, and why it is equally capable of absorbing everything of value which confronts man now and in the future.

Unfortunately, a great number of men and women are too

[1] *Unwearied Advocate,* Vol. II, p. 147.

pressed for time to study the many Papal documents, or they have little taste for the labor of searching them out and reading the full texts. For such, there is a need for an anthology such as the one presented here, whose central message we believe will have much meaning for them, and which will inspire them to work for that very wholeness of life which, paradoxically, is more realizable than ever before, and which yet seems more remote than ever before. It is hoped that many will be led to the original documents themselves. Moreover, this anthology should prove useful to editors, teachers, writers and others, in both its main body of texts, as well as in its listing of sources. Above all, this volume should contribute not a little toward increasing the popular appreciation of Papal documents, not only among Catholics, but also among non-Catholics.

One final point. There can be no satisfactory conception of things human which fails to give meaning to human sacrifice and suffering. Indeed, in the light of all that we have gone through in the past few decades, we are beginning to see that there is no truly human existence which is not based on a capacity for selflessness and for making suffering into an instrument of human fulfillment. That is why the humanism which, in its integral form, is implied by Christianity has a depth as fathomless as the human soul itself, made to the image and likeness of God. We should say it is a humanism of love, a humanism grounded on the sacrifice of the Cross. Again we can do no better than quote the Pope himself. "Look at the Cross; look at all those who have suffered! By word and example Jesus taught men; by miracles He went about doing good; but, by His Passion and Cross, He saved the world."

R. C. POLLOCK

THE MIND OF PIUS XII

NOTE

The caption which appears before each quotation serves to identify the corresponding source as given at the back of the book. It is hoped that the captions will also help to maintain interest and lend a dynamic and structural quality to the progression of quotations.

[I]

Growth and Development

Pius XII is very much concerned with the theme of growth and development, whether he is dealing with education, economics, or the social question, or with the Church herself. Regarding the Church, he has made us extremely conscious of the time dimension, stressing what he calls "a magnificent concept," that of the Church's "vital law of continuous adaptation." As to the course of history itself, he sees in it the "profound action of an intrinsic law of development," whose root is human nature, and which is carrying mankind toward a "higher unity" in international life.

Moreover, the Pope has a remarkable grasp of the complexity of historical development, for he is aware not only of "the agonizing dilemma between youth and old age" but even of the "contradictory aspects of historical evolution." Thus, he says, "In one of those evolutions full of contradictions with which history is dotted, the last centuries have seen on the one side Christian civilization being systematically menaced in its very foundation, and on the other the heritage of that civilization being ever more diffused among peoples." No one could be more sensitive than he to the paradoxical character of history, and he has expressed himself in this connection a number of times. His profound sense of history can give new courage and confidence to all who believe whole-heartedly in unchanging truth and value and who are yet not a little disturbed by the all too obvious fact of change and de-velopment.

R. C. P.

The Church's vital law of continuous adaptation

. . . the Church in her onward course watches, without pause or conflict, the divinely guided course of times and circumstances. This is the need and significance of her vital law of continuous adaptation, which some, incapable of grasping such a magnificent concept, have interpreted or described as opportunism. No; the world-embracing comprehension of the Church has nothing in common with the narrowness of a sect or with the exclusiveness of an imperialism tied to its own traditions.

The Church today and the Primitive Church

The Church of today cannot simply return to the primitive forms of the small initial flock. In her maturity, which is not old age, she holds her head high and maintains unchanged in her members the vigor of her youth. She remains necessarily what she was at her birth. She is impregnable, indestructible, invincible. She is immovable, changeless, in the writ of her foundation, sealed with the blood of the Son of God. Yet she moves, she takes new forms with the age in which she goes forward, on her way pro-gressing, yes, but not changing in her nature. . . .

(2)

No return to the past

Since these ages of its inception, the Church has developed as a living organism and has reached a higher stage of perfection, and cannot return to the days of its childhood. . . .

Development of the Church

The Church is in a position to look back with worthy pride, and unafraid, on her past and on the almost two-thousand-year-old priceless treasure of her teaching and legislation. These have increased through the fuller development and clearer understanding of the deposit of truth committed to her, as well as through the effective strengthening and perfection of her internal unity and the expansion of her liturgy, centered on the Sacrifice of the Mass and on the Sacraments, increased too by that leaven of the Christian spirit which more and more, as time passes, has come to enter into all forms and conditions of life. . . .

No retracing of steps

. . . now that her [the Church's] mission as Universal Mother of believers has attained maturity, in face of vaster needs and duties she could not without being untrue to herself retrace her steps and take on the forms of life and activity of these earlier days. . . .

The Church goes forward

No, there cannot be for the Church, whose steps God directs and accompanies through the ages, there cannot be for the human

(3)

soul, who studies history in the spirit of Christ, any going back, but only desire to go forward toward the future and to mount upwards.

The Church is in time and space

. . . Clearly the Church is also a visible society. Her life is conditioned, like the life of man, by the physical elements of time and space.

The new needs of mankind

The accomplishment of this task of regeneration, by adapting her means to the altered conditions of the times and to the new needs of the human race, is an essential and maternal office of the Church. . . .

True progress

It is, above all, a clear principle of wisdom that all progress is truly such if it knows how to add new conquests to old, to join new benefits to those acquired in the past—in a word, if it knows how to make capital of experience. . . .

Antiquity is no idol

. . . It is not wise, however, and not worthy of praise, in any way to evaluate everything by antiquity. . . .

(4)

The meaning of tradition

. . . tradition is something entirely different from mere attachment to an irretrievable past. It is exactly the opposite of reaction
against all healthy progress. Even etymologically the word is
synonymous with progress; although a synonym does not mean
that the words are identical. While progress means but the mere
fact of marching forward, step by step, looking into an uncertain
future, tradition conveys the idea of an uninterrupted march forward, which progresses both serenely and in a vital manner in
accordance with the laws of life, and which solves the agonizing
dilemma between youth and old age. . . .

O blessed tranquillity. . . .

O blessed tranquillity, thou hast nothing in common with the
spirit of holding fixedly and obstinately, unrelenting and with
childish stubbornness, to things as they are. . . .

Eternal youth of the Church

. . . The youth of the Church is eternal, for the Church does
not grow old, changing her age as she does according to the conditions of time while she marches on to eternity. The centuries
that she has passed through are but a day, as the centuries that
lie before her are but as a day. Her youth in the days of Caesars
is the same that now speaks to us. The confidence in victory of
the primitive Church drew its life, soundness and imperturba-
bility from the words of the Master: "I have overcome the world."
(John xvi, 33.) They are words which might well have been
inscribed on the wood of His Cross, the standard of His victories.

Across the centuries

The Church today, with joy and affection, clasps the hand of the Primitive Church. Across the centuries, the goodness and winsomeness of Christ living among us never fail. . . .

Worthy of reverence and respect

. . . The liturgy of early times is undoubtedly worthy of veneration, but an ancient practice is not by reason of its antiquity alone to be considered better and more fitting, either in itself or for the new conditions of later times. More recent liturgical ceremonies are also worthy of reverence and respect, since they have come into being under the influence of the Holy Spirit that is present with the Church in every age, even to the end of time; (Cf. Matthew xxviii, 20) and they are equally the works which the unspotted Spouse of Jesus Christ uses to arouse and procure the holiness of men.

A living organism

Certainly the Church is a living organism and, therefore, in those things which pertain to the sacred liturgy it grows and develops and conforms itself to the circumstances and requirements of various times, saving and guarding nevertheless the integrity of doctrine. . . .

The human side of sacred liturgy

For the sacred liturgy is made up of human as well as of divine elements. It is obvious that the latter, since they were established by the Divine Redeemer, cannot be changed in any way by men. The former, however, can undergo changes according to the needs of various times, varying events, and the good of souls. These changes are subject to the approval of the ecclesiastical hierarchy, which is under the marvelous guidance of the Holy Spirit. Hence, there has arisen the wonderful variety of Eastern and Western rites. Thus also there has come about the progressive development by which special customs in worship and works of piety have gradually evolved, which were barely indicated in the first centuries.

Each period enriches the Church

Each period of the history of the Church has contributed to the enrichment of these sacramental rites, as, to cite examples best known to you, the Roman Missal and Ritual show clearly. From the progressive development of some of these rites one recognizes easily the care of the Church in seeking the forms most adapted to their scope. . . .

Crisis of growth

. . . Institutions, like individuals, normally pass through a crisis of growth, which may have its dangers and its disappointments. . . .

Religious organizations and changing conditions

Religious organizations best serve the needs of the times when, on occasion, without giving up their own peculiar spirit, they adapt themselves to changing conditions. . . .

Religious usages in a cultural frame

As for yourselves,[1] here are Our recommendations: in this crisis of vocations take care that the customs, the kind of life or the growth of your religious families do not constitute a barrier or a cause of failure. We refer to certain usages which, if at one time they had meaning in another cultural frame, no longer have it today, and in which a truly good and courageous girl would find nothing but obstacles to her own vocation. . . .

The times in which we live. . . .

It should nevertheless be noted that the times in which we live and their peculiar conditions have brought many modifications in the habits of society and in the activities of common life. Out of these there may arise serious difficulties which could keep men from partaking of the Divine Mysteries if the law of the Eucharistic fast is to be observed in the way in which it had to be observed up to the present time.

Continuity in the midst of change

. . . It is true indeed that, as time goes on, conditions of life change. But there is never a complete break or a complete discontinuity between the law of yesterday and that of today, between the disappearance of old powers and constitutions and the appearance of a new order. In any case, whatever be the change or the transformation, the scope of every social life remains identical, sacred, obligatory; it is the development of the personal values of man as the image of God. . . .

[1] To women's religious orders.

Continuity of past, present and future

. . . Continuity in time had always appeared essential to life in society, and it seemed that this could not be conceived if men were isolated from the past, present and future. Now this is precisely the disturbing phenomenon of which we are today witnesses.

Too often of the past hardly anything is any longer known, or, at most, only what is sufficient to guess at its hazy outlines in the accumulation of its ruins.

The present is, for many, only the disordered rush of a torrent, which carries men like drift on its headlong course to the dark night of a future in which they will lose themselves with the stream that bears them on.

Contradictory aspects of historical evolution

In one of those evolutions full of contradictions with which history is dotted, the last centuries have seen on the one side Christian civilization being systematically menaced in its very foundation, and on the other the heritage of that civilization being ever more diffused among peoples. Europe and the other continents are still living, to a varying degree, by the vital forces and principles which the heritage of Christian thought has infused into them by a kind of spiritual blood-transfusion.

Different social structures

In its 2,000-year history the Church has had to live in the midst of the most diverse social structures, from the ancient one with its slavery to the modern economic system marked by the words capitalism and proletariat. . . .

Never petrified

. . . If, in particular ages or places, one or another ethnical group or social class has more than others made its influence on the Church felt, this does not mean that she becomes vassal to anyone, or is so to speak, petrified at some historical moment and debarred from any further development.

A progressive realization

. . . The Christian order, since its purpose is peace, is essentially an order of liberty. It is the cooperative effort of men and peoples toward the progressive realization in all spheres of life of the ends which God has assigned to humanity. . . .

Evolution of humanism

. . . Humanism is now the order of the day. Without doubt, there is a great difficulty in forming and recognizing, through its historic evolution, a clear concept of its nature. . . .

An intrinsic law of development

. . . The clear fact that relations between individuals of various nations and between nations themselves are growing in multiplicity and intensity makes daily more urgent a right ordering of international relations, both private and public; all the more so since this mutual drawing together is caused not only by vastly improved technological progress and by free choice but also by the more profound action of an intrinsic law of development.

A manysided approach

. . . In truth, it is impossible to solve the problem of a world political organization without being willing to leave the beaten path from time to time, without appealing to the witness of history, to a sane social philosophy, and even to a certain divining of the creative imagination.

A new situation

The relations between agriculture and industry within the single national economies, and of those latter with the economy of other nations, the manner and extent that each nation is to share in the world market—all these difficult problems present themselves today afresh and under aspects different from those of previous times. . . .

Social evolution and workers' fulfillment

It is only a progressive and prudent evolution, full of courage and in conformity with nature, enlightened and guided by the Christian law of justice and equity, that can lead to the fulfillment of the honorable desires and needs of the workers. . . .

Cultural evolution and human unity

. . . From the beginning of the present century, the means of locomotion in the material order, the evolution of the world in the cultural order, have brought people closer together and almost abolished distances and have increased contacts among the most heterogeneous groups. . . .

New needs—new remedies

Granted these principles, [you teachers] look then with a sure eye to the times and the hour to learn of new needs and examine new remedies. Confidently fix your gaze on that future which you will fashion with your own hands in the souls of your pupils. . . .

Appreciate the advances of each generation

. . . one must appreciate the advances each generation makes and see to it that their good results, thanks to wise and conscientious men, surpass and neutralize the evil wrought by unworthy exploiters.

[II]

The Complete Man

CATHOLIC CHRISTIANITY is in no way a negation of man's life in time and space. Far from it, for it is the very soul of a total integration, a "harmonious combination" of man's natural and supernatural life, "in an orderly development of his instincts and inclinations, his rich qualities and varied reactions." Life is "always a synthesis" Pius XII reminds us, "since the unique subject of every human activity is man himself." And the man he is talking about is "the complete man," "man as he is in the sight of God, his Creator and Redeemer, as he is in his concrete and his historical reality."

A passion for integration animates every word the Pope utters, expressing itself in a hundred different contexts. This passion is evident when he speaks of the necessity of universal love, while castigating an "icy solitude" of the heart, or when he attacks a "slothful tranquillity" because, as he tells us, referring to St. Thomas Aquinas, tranquillity and activity are not opposed, but "rather form a well-balanced pair. . . ." Again his preoccupation with integration is manifested in his statement that "True religion and profound humaneness are not rivals, they are sisters." And it is also expressed when he gives a special place in human life to an "exalted kindliness," that virtue which first blossomed in the soul of the saint and has become one of the cherished virtues of modern man. The need for a synthesis of supernatural love and "exalted kindliness" is pointed up when he couples the Christian life with "a genuine humane humanitarianism." One could go on at great length showing by citation how dear to the Pope's heart is this theme of a majestic unity of life which is synonymous with Catholicity.

R. C. P.

The Church's world mission

. . . She [the Church] must today, as never before, live her mission; she must reject more emphatically than ever that false and narrow concept of her spirituality and her interior life which would confine her, blind and mute, in the retirement of the sanctuary. . . .

No aloofness from life

. . . A supernaturalism that holds itself aloof, and especially one that keeps religion aloof, from economic and political needs and duties, as if these did not concern the Christian and the Catholic, is something unhealthy, something alien to the thinking of the Church. . . .

An anti-Christian separatism

To wish to draw an exact line of separation between religion and life, between the natural and the supernatural, between the Church and the world, as if they had nothing to do with each

other, as if the rights of God were valueless in all the manifold
realities of daily life, whether human or social, is entirely foreign
to Catholic thought and is positively anti-Christian. . . .

The Church and the complete man

. . . The Church cannot cut herself off, inert in the privacy of
her churches, and thus desert her divinely providential mission
of forming the complete man, and thereby collaborating without
rest in the construction of the solid foundations of society. . . .

The harmony of natural with supernatural life

. . . She [the Church] works on what is most intrinsic to man's
being, on man in his personal dignity as a free creature, in his
infinitely higher dignity as son of God.

This man the Church forms and educates because he alone,
complete in harmonious combination of his natural and supernatural life, in an orderly development of his instincts and inclinations, his rich qualities and varied reactions, is at the same time
the beginning and the end of life in human society, thus also the
principle of its equilibrium.

Concrete historical man

. . . Now this human being [to whom the Church applies her
spiritual healing power] is not the abstract man, nor considered
only in the order of pure nature, but the complete man as he
is in the sight of God, his Creator and Redeemer, as he is in his

concrete and historical reality, which could not be lost sight of without compromising the normal functioning of human intercourse.

The Church and human values

Without taking into account the fleeting opinions which have appeared at various periods, the Church has affirmed the value of what is human and what is in conformity with nature. Without any hesitation she has sought to develop it and place it in evidence. She does not admit that in the sight of God man is mere corruption and sin. . . .

The Catholic doctrine of Original Sin

. . . in the eyes of the Church, Original Sin did not intimately affect men's aptitudes and strength, and has left essentially intact the natural light of his intelligence and his freedom. Man endowed with this nature is undoubtedly injured and weakened by the heavy inheritance of a fallen nature, deprived of supernatural and preternatural gifts. He must make an effort to observe the natural law—this with the powerful assistance of the Grace of Christ—so that he can live as the honor of God and his dignity as man require.

The human body shares in the value of man

Revelation thus teaches us lofty truths concerning the human body which natural sciences and art of themselves are incapable of discovering, truths which confer on the body new value and a more elevated dignity, and thus greater motives for meriting respect. . . .

The Christian background of humanism

. . . although humanism claimed for a long time to be formally opposed to the Middle Ages which preceded it, it is certain that all it contains of the true, the good, the great and the eternal belongs to the spiritual world of the greatest genius of the Middle Ages, St. Thomas Aquinas.

The needs of one's brethren

. . . The love of God renders the mind responsive to the needs of one's brethren, ready to give spiritual and material aid, disposed to make every sacrifice in order that fervent and practical love may flourish again in the hearts of all.

A marvelous vision

The Apostle of the Gentiles later on makes himself the herald of this truth which associates men as brothers in one great family, when he proclaims to the Greek world that God "hath made of one, all mankind, to dwell upon the whole face of the earth, determining appointed times, and the limits of their habitation, that they should seek God." (Acts xvii, 26, 27)

A marvelous vision, which makes us see the human race in the unity of one common origin in God "one God and Father of all, Who is above all, and through all, and in us all" (Ephesians iv, 6); in the unity of nature which in every man is equally com-

posed of material body and spiritual, immortal soul; in the unity
of the immediate end and mission in the world; in the unity of
dwelling place, the earth, of whose resources all men can by
natural right avail themselves, to sustain and develop life; in the
unity of the supernatural end, God Himself, to Whom all should
tend; in the unity of means to secure that end.

Rooted in the community

. . . Without doubt, the aim of Redemption is the personal sanctification, if possible, of everyone. However, according to God's plan
of salvation the sanctification of the individual must be rooted,
bloom and bear fruit in the community in which he lives, which
itself is vivified by faith in God and by the spirit of Christ.

A life of mutual collaboration

. . . in the Church the individual members do not live for themselves alone, but also help their fellows, and all work in mutual
collaboration for their common comfort and for the more perfect
building up of the whole Body.

The banquet of fraternal love

But who can follow the path of Christian charity, which was
opened by the Apostles themselves, in the beginnings of the
Church, with the collections instituted by them at the fraternal
"agapai" or banquets, where patrician and slave sat side by side,
with the institution of deacons who were assigned to the loving
assistance of children and widows? The first rapid spread of the

Christian idea is, without any doubt, to be attributed chiefly to this lyricism of charity, which was unknown in the world before that time. . . .

"Members one of another"

. . . one should say that the more we become "members one of another," "mutually one of another," the closer we shall be united with God, with Christ; as on the other hand the more ardent the love that binds us to God and our divine Head, the closer we shall be united to each other in the bonds of charity.

The smallest acts of love

The smallest act has its reaction for good or evil. No act of love, no aspiration, is without its effect on the whole Mystical Body of Christ.

Each can contribute

In that [Mystical] Body, thanks to the Communion of Saints, no good can be done, no virtue practiced by individual members without its contributing something also to the salvation of all. . . .

An unconfined love

. . . Genuine love of the Church . . . is not satisfied with our being within this Body members one of another, mutually careful one for another, rejoicing with him who glories, suffering with him who suffers; we must also recognize as brothers of Christ according to the flesh, destined together with us to eternal salvation, those others who have not yet joined us in the body of the Church.

Inseparable loves

Corresponding to this love of God and of Christ there must be love of the neighbor. How can we claim to love the divine Redeemer, if we hate those whom He has redeemed with His precious blood, so that He might make them members of His Mystical Body? For that reason the beloved disciple warns us "If any man say: I love God, and hateth his brother, he is a liar. For he that loveth not his brother whom he seeth, how can he love God Whom he seeth not? And this commandment we have from God, that he who loveth God love also his brother." . . .

An icy solitude

. . . Of what value would be disputations on justice, on charity, on peace, if the will were already resolved to flee sacrifice, if the heart were determined to remain in icy solitude and if none were to dare to be the first to break through the barrier of dividing hate to hasten to offer a sincere embrace? All this would but render more guilty the sons of light, to whom less will be forgiven, if they have loved less. It was not with such disunity and inertia that the Church in its very beginning changed the face of the earth, spread rapidly, endured in her beneficent mission down the centuries and gained the admiration and trust of all peoples.

The true meaning of charity

. . . Charity is a word sometimes loosely used to signify any sort of benevolent and philanthropic activity, but for you charity has a sacred, consecrated meaning. Charity is different from any other human love because it is the replica of Christ's love for man. "A new commandment I give you, that you love one another: that as I have loved you, you also love one another." That is charity. . . .

Universal love

Supernatural charity is palpitating for the good of souls, for their eternal salvation, for their sanctification here below, but also for universal love which must embrace, for our part, all our fellow men: all our fellow men means men everywhere, unconditionally and unreservedly.

Love builds, hate destroys

. . . Fight hatred, hatred between nations as well as class hatred. Hatred can only destroy. Love builds. Against the forces of patience and of love that spring from faith in Christ and love for Him, irreligiousness, brutal egoism and class hatred must finally be shattered.

Justice and charity

. . . If Charity be not joined with strict and rigid justice, in a kind of brotherly bond, the eye of the mind is very easily clouded and thereby hindered, so that it does not discern the rights of another. . . .

Some boast of hate and spite

There are some unfortunately, today especially, who proudly boast of enmity, of hate and spite, as something that elevates and honors the dignity of man and his power. Let us, however, follow on after our King of peace, the while we gaze with sorrow on the pernicious consequences of that teaching. He has taught us not only to have love for those of a different nation and a different race, but to love even our enemies. While Our heart overflows with the sweetness of the Apostle's teaching We chant with him the length, the width, the height, the depth of the charity of Christ, which neither diversity of race or culture, neither the wasteless tracks of ocean, nor wars, be their cause just or unjust, can ever weaken or destroy.

We must know how to forgive

Whoever would be a sincere Christian must know how to forgive. "Thou wicked servant"—is the rebuke of the Gospel parable (Math. xviii, 32)—"was it not thy duty to have mercy on thy fellow-servant, as I had on thee?"

Soul to soul

There is another work from which no one of you should consider himself dispensed: the work of individual approach, soul to soul, everywhere, and in all circumstances. We would like no one to speak with you, deal with you, work with you, without receiving a ray of Christian light into his mind.

Reached by divers ways

One of the merits of Christianity, and an indication of its exuberant vitality, is the fact that the goal which God has fixed for every soul, namely sanctity, can be reached by divers ways. The spirit breathes how and where it wills: hence the manifold variety of saints who shine like stars in the firmament of the Church and preach the richness of divine gifts. . . .

Individual and collective egoism

. . . What calamities could be averted, what happiness and tranquillity assured, if the social and international forces working to establish peace would let themselves be permeated by the deep lessons of the Gospel of Love in their struggle against individual or collective egoism! . . .

True religion and profound humaneness. . . .

True religion and profound humaneness are not rivals. They are sisters.

They have nothing to fear from one another, but everything to gain. Let each remain loyal to the law of its being, while it respects the vital needs and varied outward manifestations of the other, and the resultant harmonizing of two forces will endow any people engaged in the fulfillment of its appointed tasks with the most valuable incentives to real prosperity and solid progress.

Christian humanitarianism

. . . There is no opposition between the laws that govern the life of faithful Christians and the postulates of a genuine humane humanitarianism, but rather unity and mutual support. . . .

Egotistical "isolationism"

A convinced Christian cannot confine himself within an easy and egotistical "isolationism," when he witnesses the needs and misery of his brothers; when pleas for help come to him from those in economic distress; when he knows the aspirations of the working classes for more normal and just conditions of life; when he is aware of the abuses of an economic system which puts money above social obligations; when he is not ignorant of the aberrations of an intransigent nationalism which denies or spurns the common bonds linking the separate nations together, and imposing on each one of them many and varied duties toward the great family of nations.

The example of Our Lord

Son of God and Herald of His heavenly kingdom, He was happy in bending compassionately over the wounds of humanity and the tattered rags of poverty. He was not satisfied with proclaiming the law of justice and charity; nor with condemning with withering anathemas the hardhearted, the inhuman, the selfish; nor with the warning that the final sentence of the Last Day will have as the norm of its judgment the exercise of charity, as the proof of the love of God. But He spent Himself personally in order to help, to heal, to feed. Certainly He did not ask whether, and to what extent, the misfortune before Him happened because the political and economic order of his time was defective or lacking. He was not indifferent to that. On the contrary, He is the Lord of the world and of its order. But just as His action as Saviour was personal, so He wished to meet life's other misfortunes with a love that was personal. The example of Jesus is today, as every day, a strict duty for all.

Stronger than death

. . . Whoever lives by the spirit of Christ refuses to let himself be beaten down by the difficulties which oppose him, but on the contrary feels himself impelled to work with all his strength and with the fullest confidence in God. He does not draw back before the straits and the necessities of the moment but faces their severity ready to give aid with that love which flees no sacrifice, is stronger than death, and will not be quenched by the rushing waters of tribulation.

A slothful tranquillity

. . . for a Christian who is conscious of his responsibilities even toward the least of his brethren, there is no such thing as slothful tranquillity; nor is there question of flight, but of struggle, of action against every inaction and desertion in the great spiritual combat where the stakes are the construction, nay the very soul, of the society of tomorrow.

(25)

At the threshold of life

Through the languishing of faith in men's hearts, through the pleasure-seeking that molds and captivates their lives, men are driven to judge as evil and as unmixed evil the physical mishaps of this earth. They have forgotten that suffering stands at the threshold of life as the way that leads to the smiles of the cradle; they have forgotten that it is more often than not the shadow of the Cross of Calvary thrown on the path of the Resurrection. . . .

Lesson of the Cross

. . . Look at the Cross; look at all those who have suffered! By word and example Jesus taught men; by miracles He went about doing good; but, by His Passion and Cross, He saved the world: *"Adoramus te, Christe, et benedicimus tibi, quia per Crucem tuam redemisti mundum."* (We adore Thee, O Christ, and we bless Thee, because by Thy Cross Thou hast redeemed the world.) The same Jesus, beckoning you to carry your cross and to follow Him, asks you at the same time to be a fellow-worker with Him in the redemption of the world. . . .

Faith and limitless dimensions

Beloved sons and daughters! If to your eyes, wearied with sickness, the whole universe, gloomy and oppressive, is confined within the narrow space of a little room, let in the light of faith, and at once that universe will regain its limitless dimensions. . . .

The economy of salvation

. . . Do you [the sick] want to transform yourself into Him? Do you want to be a channel of life for Him? In sickness you can find the cross, be nailed to it and thus die to yourself so that He may live and make use of you. How many of you, beloved children, would like to help Jesus save souls? Then offer Him your sufferings according to all the intentions for which He continually offers Himself on the altars of our churches. . . . And on the day on which the mystery of Providence in the economy of salvation will be revealed in Heaven, you will at last see to what extent the world of the healthy is your debtor.

Trust in God means. . . .

Trust in God means the abandonment of oneself, with all the force of the will sustained by grace and love, in spite of all the doubts suggested by appearances to the contrary, to the wisdom and the infinite love of God. It means believing that nothing in this world escapes His providence, whether in the universal or in the particular order; that nothing great or small happens which is not foreseen, wished or permitted, directed always by Providence to Its exalted ends. . . .

A glorious fusion

Clarity of vision, devotion, courage, inventive genius, and the sense of brotherly love in all upright and honest men determine the measure and extent to which Christian thought will succeed in maintaining and supporting the gigantic work of restoration in social, economic and international life through a plan that does not conflict with the religious and moral content of Christian civilization.

The Church elevates human energies

... She [the Church] does not suppress human energies but lifts them up to all that is noble and generous and forms characters which do not compromise with conscience. Nor has she who civilizes the nations ever retarded the civil progress of mankind, at which on the contrary she is pleased and glad with a mother's pride. ...

Renewal of all human action

The Holy Spirit will make you see very clearly this above all, that no field of human activity can be withdrawn from Christ's action of renewal: through Whom and in Whom all things are. ...

Men must recognize that the Gospel has the task of completely leavening the thought of mankind, and if there are still some who doubt the necessity of a radical transformation in a Christian sense, you must remind them that human activity in all its manifestations, speculative as well as external, hence also even artistic activity, should have a Christian inspiration, and cannot escape the impact of the thought and grace of Christ.

The single measure of real progress

... For the sovereign Judge who awaits us at the threshold of eternity when life is ended warns us all, high and low, to make careful use of the gifts received from God, to avoid all injustice and to profit by every opportunity to love and to do good. That is the single measure of all real progress; for progress is genuine and not artificial only when it is also a step toward God and His likeness. . . .

The Christian religion and life here below

. . . it is indeed true that religion has its laws and institutions for eternal happiness but it is also undeniable that it dowers life here below with so many benefits that it could do no more even if the principal reason for its existence were to make men happy during the brief span of their earthly life.

Obedience to God and human tranquillity

. . . To diminish the obedience due to the Divine Creator, to regulate it out of existence, is thus nothing else than to throw into confusion and to break up entirely the tranquillity of the individual citizen's life, of the life of the family, of the separate nations and, ultimately, of the whole human race. . . .

Life is always a synthesis

An effort is sometimes made to justify the emancipation from morality of external human activities—such as the sciences, politics and art—on philosophic grounds, on the basis of the autonomy which belongs to them in their particular spheres, of being governed according to their own laws; though it is admitted that these generally agree with the moral laws. As an example, art is brought forward: in its regard, not only is every dependence but also every relation with morality denied with the dictum that art is purely art and not morality or anything else; hence it is to be ruled solely by the laws of aesthetics (which, however, if they are truly such, will not pander to concupiscence). The same, it is said, holds for politics and economics, which have no need of seeking counsel from other sciences, including ethics: guided by their own laws, they are said by that very fact to be good and just.

As is obvious, this is a subtle way of withdrawing conscience from the rule of the moral law. In fact, it cannot be denied that such autonomy is just, in so far as it expresses the distinctive methods of each activity and the limits which theoretically separate their diverse forms; but the separation of method should not mean that the scientist, the artist, the politician, are free from moral solicitude in the exercise of their activity, especially if this has repercussions in the ethical field, as have art, politics and economics. The clear-cut theoretical separation has no sense in life, which is always a synthesis, since the unique subject of every kind of activity is man himself, whose free and deliberate acts cannot escape moral evaluation.

[III]

The Social Question

IUS XII understands man's longing for a society "more in harmony with the exigencies of human nature." The misery of the world, he reminds us, springs from the fact that it is lacking in both humanity and Christianity. And against every degradation of social life which would reduce man to the status of a mere object to be exploited, the Pope affirms the principle that "as regards the end of the social economy, every productive member is the subject and not the object of economic life." Needless to say, this principle applies with full force to society as a whole and not only to the economy.

Basing itself on the natural law within the framework of Christianity, the Church's social doctrine can support neither economic individualism nor collectivism, for each violates the dignity of the human person and the order of values. Apart from the principles of Catholic social doctrine, no sound social program can be envisaged. But these principles must be applied in each concrete situation according to its special circumstances and in line with knowledge, experience and technical possibilities. Were we to hold fast to these principles and to the Christian spirit infusing them, we should certainly bring closer the day when society will be truly communal, in centering itself around the human person, viewed in his integral life.

The Pope speaks often of the need for an organic concept of society rather than a mechanical one, since men must be united from within as well as from without. But such an organic and interior unity is unthinkable in the absence of genuine religious life.

R. C. P.

Longing for a new world

The hands of the clock of history are now pointing to an hour both grave and decisive for all mankind. An old world lies in fragments. To see arise as quickly as possible from those ruins a new world, healthier, juridically better organized, more in harmony with the exigencies of human nature; such is the longing of its tortured peoples.

A total transformation of society

It is an entire world which must be rebuilt from its foundations, transformed from savage to human, from human to divine, that is to say, according to the heart of God. . . .

A social challenge

. . . The whole complex structure of society is in need of adjustment and improvement, thoroughly shaken as it is in its foundations.

The wound of our society

. . . The wound of our individualistic and materialistic society will not be healed, the deep chasm will not be bridged, by no matter what system, if the system itself is materialistic in principle and mechanical in practice.

The great misery of the social order. . . .

The great misery of the social order is that it is neither deeply Christian nor really human, but solely technical and economic. It is not built on what should be its real basis and the solid foundation of its unity—the common character which men possess by their nature and by being sons of God through the grace of divine adoption.

The Church's authority and the social question

It was in the profound conviction that the Church has not only the right but even the duty to make an authoritative pronouncement on the social question, that Leo XIII addressed his message to the world. He had no intention of laying down guiding principles on the purely practical, we might say technical side of the social structure; for he was well aware of the fact—as Our immediate predecessor of saintly memory Pius XI pointed out ten years ago in his commemorative Encyclical, *Quadragesimo Anno*—that the Church does not claim such a mission. . . .

It is, on the other hand, the indisputable competence of the Church, on that side of the social order where it meets and enters into contact with the moral order, to decide whether the bases of a given social system are in accord with the unchangeable order which God our Creator and Redeemer has shown us through the Natural Law and Revelation, that two-fold manifestation to which Leo XIII appeals in his Encyclical. . . .

No other solution

. . . There is no other solution for humanity but to build the world anew in the spirit of Christ. He alone, in truth, is the Saviour of the individual, the family, society as a whole. . . .

Solution of the social question

. . . Without the Church the social question is insoluble. But neither can she solve it alone. She needs the collaboration of the intellectual, economic and technical resources of leaders in public life.

Society and the person

The origin and the primary scope of social life is the conservation, development and perfection of the human person, helping him to realize accurately the demands and values of religion and culture set by the Creator for every man and for all mankind, both as a whole and in its natural ramifications.

The community exists for man

. . . It must be noted that, in his personal being, man is not finally ordered to his usefulness to society. On the contrary, the community exists for man.

The community is the great means intended by nature and God to regulate the exchange of mutual needs and to aid each man to develop his personality fully according to his individual and social abilities.

The development of personal values

The precise, bedrock, basic rules that govern society cannot be prejudiced by the intervention of human agency. They can be denied, overlooked, despised, transgressed, but they can never be overthrown with legal validity. It is true indeed that, as time goes on, conditions of life change. But there is never a complete break or a complete discontinuity between the law of yesterday and that of today, between the disappearance of old powers and constitutions and the appearance of a new order. In any case, whatever be the change or transformation, the scope of every social life remains identical, sacred, obligatory; it is the development of the personal values of man as the image of God; and the obligation remains with every member of the human family to realize his unchangeable destiny, whosoever be the legislator and the authority whom he obeys.

The natural law and social doctrine

The natural law—here is the foundation on which the social doctrine of the Church rests. It is precisely her Christian conception of the world which has inspired and sustained the Church in building up this doctrine on such a foundation. When she struggles to win and defend her own freedom, she is actually doing this for the true freedom and for the fundamental rights of man. In her eyes these essential rights are so inviolable that no argument of State and no pretext of common good can prevail against them.

A presupposition to religious growth

. . . It is well known that the normal growth and increase of religious life presupposes a certain measure of healthy economic and social conditions. Who can resist a pang of emotion upon seeing how economic misery and social evils render Christian life according to the commands of God more difficult and too often demand heroic sacrifices? . . .

Wealth and poverty

. . . The contrast between wealth and poverty, which is intolerable to the Christian conscience, is brought home to you most strongly by the picture of present conditions in the world. You propose to find some remedy for it through the increase and better distribution of national income.

A more just distribution of wealth

. . . For Catholics the path to be followed in the social question is clearly outlined in the doctrine of the Church: the blessing of God will descend on your work if you do not swerve in the slightest degree from this path. You have no need to think out apparent solutions or to gain by facile and empty formulae results that prove only a delusion. What you can and ought to strive for, is a more just distribution of wealth. This is and this remains a central point in Catholic social doctrine.

Woe to him. . . .

. . . Woe to him who forgets that a true national economy incorporates social justice and demands a just and fitting sharing by all in the goods of the country. . . .

Justice requires. . . .

. . . Justice requires that all men acknowledge and defend the sacrosanct rights of human freedom and human dignity, and that the infinite wealth and resources with which God has endowed the whole of the earth, shall be distributed, in conformity with right reason, for the use of all His children. . . .

Purpose of the national economy

. . . the national economy, as it is the product of the men who work together in the community of the State, has no other end than to secure without interruption the material conditions in which the individual life of the citizens may fully develop. . . .

The basic idea. . . .

. . . In Our Encyclical *Sertum Laetitiae* directed to the bishops of the United States of America, We called the attention of all to the basic idea of these principles [on the question of property and man's sustenance] which consists, as We said, in the assertion of the unquestionable need "That the goods, which were created by God for all men, should flow equally to all, according to the principles of justice and charity."

The true economic wealth of a people

The purpose of the economic and social organism, as we must recall, is to obtain for its members and their families all the goods that the resources of nature and of industry, as well as a social organization of economic life, are capable of obtaining for them. . . .

If it is true that the best and most natural means of satisfying this obligation is to increase available goods through a healthy development of production, it is still necessary, in pursuing this effort, to have care to distribute justly the fruit of the labor of all. "If such a just distribution of goods were not realized or were only imperfectly assured, the genuine aim of the national economy would not have been realized, since however great the abundance of available goods might be, if the people are not allowed to share in them, they would still be not rich but poor" (Radio Message, June 1, 1941).

Social revolution

. . . The Church has never preached social revolution; but always and everywhere, from the Epistle of St. Paul to Philemon to the social teaching of the Popes of the 19th and 20th centuries, she has worked hard to have more concern shown for the human being than for economic and technical advantages, and to get as many as possible, on their part, to do all they can to live the Christian life and one worthy of a human being.

Marxist Socialism

Always moved by religious motives, the Church has condemned the various forms of Marxist Socialism; and she condemns them today, because it is her permanent right and duty to safeguard men from currents of thought and influences that jeopardize their eternal salvation. But the Church cannot ignore or overlook the fact that the worker in his efforts to better his lot, is opposed by a machinery which is not only not in accordance with nature, but is at variance with God's plan and with the purpose He had in creating the goods of earth.

A false concept of private property

The Christian conscience cannot admit as just a social order which either denies in principle or renders impossible or nega-tory in practice, the natural right to property whether over con-sumptive goods or by means of production. But neither can it accept those systems which recognize the right to private property according to a completely false concept of it and which are there-fore opposed to a true and healthy social order.

Accordingly where, for instance, "Capitalism" is based on such false concepts and arrogates to itself an unlimited right over prop-erty, without any subordination to the common good, the Church has condemned it as contrary to the natural law. In fact, We see the ever-increasing ranks of the workers frequently confronted with this excessive concentration of economic goods which, often hid-den under anonymous titles, are successfully withdrawn from con-tributing, as they should, to the social order, and place the worker in a situation where it is virtually impossible for him effectively to acquire private property of his own. We see the small and me-dium holdings diminish and lose their value in human society, and constrained to join in a conflict ever more difficult and with-out hope of success.

A fatal error

After the fateful economy of the past decades, during which the lives of all citizens were subordinated to the stimulus of gain, there now succeeds another and no less fateful policy which, while it considers everything with reference to the State, excludes all thought of ethics or religion. This is a fatal travesty, a fatal error. It is calculated to bring about far-reaching consequences for social life, which is never nearer to losing its noblest prerogatives than when it thinks it can deny or forget with impunity the external source of its own dignity: God.

The desire for gain versus human needs

. . . As Our glorious Predecessor, Pius XI, has so effectively shown in his Encyclical *Quadragesimo Anno,* it happens too often that human needs do not, in accordance with natural and objective importance, rule economic life and the use of capital. On the contrary, capital and its desire for gain determine what the needs of man should be and to what extent they are to be satisfied. Therefore, it is not human labor in the service of the common welfare that attracts capital to it and presses it into service. Rather, capital tosses labor and man himself here and there like a ball in a game. . . .

The degradation of man

. . . The goods of the earth, whose exchange ought to stabilize and maintain economic equilibrium among nations, have become the object of political speculation. This applies not only to material goods, but alas! to man also. He has, in many instances, been reduced to the level of a commodity to be exploited.

Man is more important. . . .

Every plan or program must be inspired by the principle that man as subject, guardian and promoter of human values, is more important than mere things, is more important than practical applications of scientific progress. . . .

The violences of an egoistic economy

The social question, beloved sons, is undoubtedly an economic question also, but even more than that it is a question which concerns the ordered regulation of human society. And, in its deepest sense, it is a moral and, therefore, a religious question. As such it may be summed up thus: have men—from the individual to the people, and right through to the community of peoples—the moral strength to create such public conditions that in the life of society there will not be any individuals or any peoples who are merely objects, that is to say, deprived of all right and exposed to exploitation by others, but all instead will be subjects, that is, having a legitimate share in the formation of the social order, and able, according to their art or profession, to live happily and tranquilly with sufficient means of support, protected effectively against the violences of an egoistic economy, in freedom defined by the general welfare, and with full human dignity, each respecting his neighbor as he respects himself?

Human values above quantitative considerations

. . . One must no longer consider the standard of living and employment of labor as purely quantitative factors, but rather as human values in the full sense of the word.

(41)

The first and fundamental right

Every man, as a living being gifted with reason, has in fact from nature the fundamental right to make use of the material goods of the earth, while it is left to the will of man and to the juridical statutes of nations to regulate in greater detail the actuation of this right. This individual right cannot in any way be suppressed, even by other clear and undisputed rights over material goods. Undoubtedly the natural order, deriving from God, demands also private property and the free reciprocal commerce of goods by interchange and gift, as well as the functioning of the State as a control over both these institutions. But all this remains subordinated to the natural scope of material goods and cannot emancipate itself from the first and fundamental right which concedes their use to all men; but it should rather serve to make possible the actuation of this right in conformity with its scope. . . .

Socialization

The Catholic Associations support socialization only in cases where it appears really necessary for the common welfare; in other words, when it is the only means to remedy an injustice and to ensure the coordinated use of the same forces to the benefit of the economic life of the nation, so that the normal and peaceful development of that economic life may open the gates to material prosperity for all, a prosperity which may become a sound foundation for the development of cultural and religious life. In any case, the Associations recognize that socialization carries with it the obligation of fitting compensation, such as in concrete circumstances is just and fair to those concerned. As for "the democratization of economy" it is equally endangered by monopolies—that is, by the economic tyranny of an anonymous conglomeration of private capital—and by the preponderant power of organized masses, ready to use their power to the detriment of justice and the rights of others.

State ownership and management

. . . There can be no question that the Church also admits—within certain just limits—state ownership and management, judging that "certain forms of property may legitimately be reserved to the public authority: those which represent a dominating power so great that it cannot without danger to the general welfare be entrusted to private individuals" (*Quadragesimo Anno*). But to make of this state enterprise the normal rule for public economic organization would mean reversing the order of things. Actually it is the mission of public law to serve private rights, not to absorb them. The economy is not of its nature—not more, for that matter, than any other human activity—a state institution. It is, on the contrary, the living product of the free initiative of individuals and of their freely established associations.

Business and the national economy

Those who set about treating questions relating to the reform of the structure of industry without taking into account that every single business is by its own purpose closely tied to the whole of the national economy, run the risk of laying down erroneous and false premises with danger to the entire economic and social order. . . .

The State and private property

The social and economic policy of the future, the controlling power of the State, of local bodies, of professional institutions cannot permanently secure their end, which is the genuine productivity of social life and the normal returns on national economy, except by respecting and safeguarding the vital function of private property in its personal and social values. When the distribution of property is an obstacle to this end—which is not necessarily nor always an outcome of the extension of private inheritance—the State may in the public interest, intervene by regulating its use or even, if it cannot equitably meet the situation in any other way, by decreeing the expropriation of property, giving a suitable indemnity.

For the same purpose small and medium holdings in agriculture, in the arts and trades, in commerce and industry should be guaranteed and promoted: cooperative unions should ensure for them the advantages of big business; where big business even today shows itself more productive, there should be given the possibility of tempering the labor contract with a contract of co-ownership (Encycl. *Quadragesimo Anno*).

A new basis for economic organization

The time has come to repudiate empty phrases, and to attempt to organize the forces of the people on a new basis; to raise them above the distinction between employers and would-be workers, and to realize that higher unity which is a bond between all those who co-operate in production, formed by their solidarity in the duty of working together for the common good and filling together the needs of the community. If this solidarity is extended to all branches of production, if it becomes the foundation for a better economic system it will lead the working classes to obtain honestly their share of responsibility in the direction of the national economy. . . .

An organic concept of society

Order, which is fundamental in an association of men (of beings, that is, who strive to attain an end appropriate to their nature) is not a merely external linking up of parts which are numerically distinct. It is rather, and must be, a tendency and an ever more perfect approach to an internal union; and this does not exclude differences founded in fact and sanctioned by the Will of God or by supernatural standards.

Organic unity

. . . There can be no natural organic unity among those engaged in production so long as quantitative utilitarianism—the consideration of maximum profitability—is the sole norm which determines the location of plants and the distribution of work, so long as the concept of "class" artificially divides men in Society, and there no longer exists a spirit of cooperation within occupational groups.

Public authorities and coordination

. . . although the public authorities should not substitute their oppressive omnipotence for the legitimate independence of private initiatives, these authorities have, in this matter, an undeniable function of coordination, which is made even more necessary by the confusion of present conditions, especially social conditions. . . .

An integral economic policy

. . . Specifically, without the cooperation of the public authorities
it is not possible to formulate an integral economic policy which
would promote active cooperation on the part of all and an increase
of industrial production—direct source of national income. . . .

Workers and the national economy

. . . if both employers and workers have a common interest in the
healthy prosperity of the national economy, why should it not be
legitimate to give to the workers a just share of responsibility in
the organization and development of that economy? This remark,
which We made in Our address of May 7, 1949, is all the more
opportune now when, under the difficulties, insecurities and joint
liabilities which mark the present time, a country must sometimes
make economic decisions which will affect the whole future of
the national community and often even the future of the whole
family of nations.

Human society must remain human

. . . Human society is not a machine, and must not be made such,
not even in the economic field. . . .

The concept of the machine dominates

. . . modern society, which wishes to plan and organize all things,
comes into conflict, since it is conceived as a machine, with that

which is living, and which therefore cannot be subjected to quantitative calculations. . . .

Technical progress and the general good

. . . Technical progress does not determine economic life as a fatal and necessary factor. It has indeed too often yielded timidly to the demands of rapacious, selfish plans calculated to accumulate capital indefinitely; why should it not then yield also to the necessity of maintaining and ensuring private property for all, that cornerstone of social order? Even technical progress, as a social factor, should not prevail over the general good, but should rather be directed and subordinated to it.

Tormenting the conscience

. . . Those who uphold an impersonal idea of society condemn to interior torment the very conscience on which depends in great part moral renovation and salvation. And this perhaps is the widest deviation from the Divine plan that man reaches in his efforts to help his fellow man. . . .

A spirit of cold calculation

. . . an organization animated by a spirit of cold calculation, while trying to compress life within the narrow framework of a chart, as though it were something static, becomes the negation of, and an outrage to, life itself and to the essential characteristic of life, which is its incessant dynamism, communicated to it by nature and manifested in the immensely diversified scale of particular circumstances.

Blindness to human dignity

The great temptation of an age that calls itself social—when, besides the Church, the State, the municipality and other public bodies devote themselves so much to social problems—is that when the poor man knocks on the door, people, even believers, will just send him away to an agency or social center, to an organization, thinking that their personal obligation has been sufficiently fulfilled by their contributions in taxes or voluntary gifts to those institutions.

A challenge to the American people

What a proud vaunt it will be for the American people, by nature inclined to grandiose undertakings and to liberality, if they untie the knotty and difficult social question by following the sure paths illuminated by the light of the Gospel and thus lay the basis of a happier age! If this is to come to pass power must not be dissipated through disunion but rather strengthened through harmony. . . .

[IV]

The Modern State

THE HOLY FATHER has repeatedly warned us against the threat of the omnipotent state. The state does not exist to crush the autonomy of individuals and social groups. On the contrary, its function is to safeguard and promote the convergence of all activities to a common good in conformity with the natural law, the true common good as against its false imitation. However, as he has declared a number of times, even if conceived properly, the state, under modern conditions, cannot perform its functions without the enlargement of its sphere of rights and its activities. It is particularly instructive to find the Pope excoriating, not only totalitarianism, but authoritarianism as well, which many have falsely identified with the Church, despite the fact that it is a political concept.

In an eloquent statement of the way in which Christianity proved to be a liberating force in the political order, he points out how the doctrine of the human immortal soul created to the image of its Maker gave man "an inherent dignity and rights that no earthly power dare challenge in justice." "Such teaching," he concludes, "could not but seem revolutionary to Nero and to every despot down the years; it awakened a realization that man has certain liberties independent of the State. It was revolutionary, no doubt."

R. C. P.

True concept of the State

. . . What, therefore, is the true concept of the State if not that of a moral organism based on the moral order of the world? The State is not an omnipotence crushing all legitimate autonomy. Instead, its function, its magnificent function, consists in favoring, helping and promoting an intimate coalition, an active cooperation aimed at a higher unity of members who, while respecting their subordination to the purpose of the State, contribute in the most effective manner to the welfare of the whole community, precisely insofar as they preserve and develop their individual and natural character. Neither the individual nor the family should be absorbed by the State. Each one retains and should protect his liberty of movement to the extent that he does not tend to prejudice the common good.

A false common good

. . . individuals—each and every one—and families have certain rights and liberties which the State must always protect; which it must never violate or sacrifice to a pretended common good. We have in mind, to cite a few examples, the right to honor and to a good reputation, the right and the freedom to worship the true God, the inherently primary right of parents over their children and their children's education. The fact that some recent constitutions have adopted this conception is a happy omen which we joyfully acclaim as the dawn of a renewal of respect for the true rights of man, such as they have been willed and established by God.

The State and the rights of the person

. . . Civic society is also of Divine origin and indicated by nature itself; but it is subsequent to man and meant to be a means to defend him and to help him in the legitimate exercise of his God-given rights. Once the state, to the exclusion of God, makes itself the source of the rights of the human person, man is forthwith reduced to the condition of a slave, of a mere civic commodity to be exploited for the selfish aims of a group that happens to have power. . . .

The essential task

To safeguard the inviolable sphere of the rights of the human person and to facilitate the fulfillment of his duties should be the essential office of every public authority. Does not this flow from that genuine concept of the common good which the State is called upon to promote? . . .

The State and the common good

. . . it is the noble prerogative and function of the State to control, aid and direct the private and individual activities of national life that they converge harmoniously toward the common good. That good can neither be defined according to arbitrary ideas nor can it accept for its standard primarily the material prosperity of society, but rather it should be defined according to the harmonious de-

velopment and the natural perfection of man. It is for this perfection that society is designed by the Creator as a means.

The goal of political and economic activity

Reason, enlightened by faith, assigns to individuals and to
particular societies in the social organization a definite and exalted
place. It knows, to mention only the most important, that the
whole political and economic activity of the state is directed to
the permanent realization of the common good.

An organic and organizing unity

The State does not contain in itself and does not mechanically
bring together in a given territory a shapeless mass of individuals.

It is and should be in practice the organic and organizing unity
of a real people. The people and a shapeless multitude (or, as it is
called, "the masses") are two distinct concepts.

Totalitarianism, a mechanical unity

It is undeniable that one of the vital exigencies of every human
community, hence also of the Church and the State, consists in
the permanent assurance of unity in the diversity of their members.

Now "totalitarianism" is utterly incapable of providing for this
need, because it extends the civil power beyond due limits; it
determines and fixes, both in substance and form, every field of
activity, and thus compresses all legitimate manifestation of life—
personal, local and professional—into a mechanical unity of collectivity under the stamp of nation, race, or class.

Authoritarianism versus true community

The fundamental exigency [for unity] which has been mentioned is also far from being satisfied by that other concept of civil authority, which may be called "authoritarianism," because it excludes the citizens from all effective participation in or influence upon the formation of the will of the society. Consequently it splits the nation into two categories, the rulers and the ruled, and the relations between the two are either purely mechanical as the result of force or have no more than a biological basis.

The "common good" of authoritarianism

Who can fail to see that this [authoritarianism] is a complete perversion of the true nature of the power of the State? For this power, both in itself and through the exercise of its functions, must tend to make of the State a true community, intimately united in a final purpose which is the common good. But in this system the concept of the common good is so unsubstantial and is so obviously but a mask for the unilateral interests of the ruler, that an unrestrained "dynamism" on the part of the law-making power excludes all juridical security and so destroys a basic element of every true judicial order.

Such a false dynamism could not fail to submerge and destroy the essential rights which are acknowledged as belonging to physical and moral persons in the Church. . . .

"Authoritarianism" and the Church

. . . The nature of ecclesiastical authority has nothing in common with this "authoritarianism"; the latter can claim no point of resemblance to the hierarchical constitution of the Church.

Cooperation in the whole life of the State

. . . In the eyes of the Church no other social institution, after the family, is so vitally and essentially necessary as the State. It has its roots in the order of creation and is, itself, one of the constituent elements of the natural law.

This is the reason why cooperation in the formation of the State and in the organization of its functions assumes such primary importance. This cooperation certainly involves a special and far-reaching coordination of effort for the welfare of humanity. . . .

An expansion of rights

. . . No one of good will and vision will think of refusing the State, in the exceptional conditions of the world of today, correspondingly wider and exceptional rights to meet the popular needs. But even in such emergencies, the moral law, established by God, demands that the lawfulness of each such measure and its real necessity be scrutinized with the greatest rigor according to the standards of the common good.

Widening its field of activity

. . . For, in the tangled confusion of existing conditions, especially social conditions, no one doubts the necessity for the State to widen its field of activity and also to increase its power.

This expansion could be without real danger, if clear knowledge and exact appreciation of the real importance of the role and of the purpose of the State had progressed in the same ratio. . . .

State planning

The present era witnesses a luxuriant blossoming of "plans" and "unifications." We recognize willingly that, within legitimate limits, these can be desirable and even required by circumstances, and, once more, what We condemn is but the excessive seizure of power by the State.

Sacrifices for the common good

Those people who do not wish to see themselves condemned to remain behind in the material and cultural field cannot refrain from the necessity of seeking and finding a reply to and a solution of the urgent problems of the new times, with their economic, political and social repercussions. For the realization of these ends, the power of the State often is obliged to ask all classes of people to make heavy sacrifices for the common good.

Loss of respect for the common good

. . . In some countries, the modern state is becoming a gigantic administrative machine. It extends its influence over almost every phase of life. It would bring under its administration the entire gamut of political, economic, social and intellectual life from birth to death.

No wonder, then, if in this impersonal atmosphere, which tends to penetrate and pervade all human life, respect for the common good becomes dormant in the conscience of individuals, and the state loses more and more its primary character of a community of morally responsible citizens.

Here may be recognized the origin and source of that phenomenon which is submerging modern man under its tide of anguish: his "depersonalization." In large measure his identity and name have been taken from him; in many of the more important activities of life he has been reduced to a mere material object of society, while society itself has been transformed into an impersonal system and into a cold organization of force.

The last word belongs to those. . . .

. . . who does not realize the damage which would result, under the circumstances [State planning], should the last word in affairs of the State be reserved to mere organizational technicians? No, the last word belongs to those who see in the State a living being, a normal emanation from human nature. It belongs to those who govern, in the name of the State, not man immediately, but the affairs of the country in such a way that individuals never find themselves, either in their private or social lives, submerged under the weight of State administration. The last word belongs to those for whom the natural law is more than a purely negative norm, more than a frontier closed to the infiltration of positive legislation, and more than a simple technical adjustment to contingencies. It belongs rather to those who respect the natural law as the soul of this positive legislation—a soul which gives it its form, its meaning, its life. May the last word, the decisive word, in the administration of public affairs be the prerogative of such men.

Blind worship of numbers

. . . at the present time the life of nations is everywhere disintegrated by the blind worship of numerical strength. The citizen is the voter. But, as such, he is in reality nothing but one of the units, the total of which constitutes a majority or a minority, which the shifting of a few votes or even of a single one would suffice to reverse. As far as parties are concerned, he is of importance only for his voting value, that is, the support which his vote provides. No concern is shown for his position and role in his family and his profession.

The single individual today

. . . That people must bear their collective lot there is no doubt, but where responsibility is concerned, the structure of the modern State machine, the almost inseparable interlocking of economic and political relations, do not allow the simple individual to intervene effectively in political decisions. At the most, he can influence the general orientation by his free vote, but again only to a limited degree.

Manipulation of the "masses"

By deft management and employment the State can also utilize the elementary power of the masses. In the ambitious hands of one or of many who have been artificially brought together for selfish aims, the "masses" who have been reduced to the minimum status of a mere machine can be used by the state to impose its whims on the better part of the real people. Thus the common welfare is injured seriously and for a long while, and the injury is often hard to heal.

Function of the juridical order

That social life, such as God willed it, may attain its scope, it needs a juridical order to support it from without, to defend and protect it. The function of this juridical order is not to dominate but to serve, to help the development and the increase of society's vitality in the rich multiplicity of its ends, leading all the individual energies to their perfection in peaceful competition, and defending them with appropriate and honest means against all that may militate against their full evolution.

Such an order, that it may safeguard the equilibrium, the safety and the harmony of society, has also the power of coercion against those, who only by this means can be held within the noble discipline of social life.

Respect and obedience

. . . justice requires that to lawfully constituted authority there be given that respect and obedience which is its due; that the laws which are made shall be in wise conformity with the common good; and that, as a matter of conscience, all men shall render obedience to these laws. . . .

The normal man serves as rule

. . . let us not gloss over the plain fact that man is a personal being, endowed with intelligence and free will, who decides finally himself what he will do or not do. This does not mean that he is free from every internal or external influence, from every inclination and attraction. . . But it does mean that, despite all the obstacles, the normal man can and must assert his will; and it is the normal man who must serve as the rule for society and law.

Penal law would have no sense if it did not take into consideration this aspect of man, but penal law makes complete sense because this aspect is true. And since this aspect of man, personal

and free, is a conviction of humanity, the effort to establish a
uniform penal code has a solid basis.

The law and human nature

The law is ultimately founded on the stable and immutable
nature of things. Wherever there are men and nations gathered
in communities with laws, are they not precisely human beings
with a nature which is essentially the same? The needs which
derive from that nature are the guide-rules of law. However different the formulation given to these needs in positive law, according to various times and places or varying degrees of development
and culture, their central kernel is always the same, because it is
the expression of man's nature.

Positive law

. . . Those needs [which derive from human nature] are, as it
were, the dead point of a pendulum. Positive law swings beyond
the dead point, now on one side, now on the other, but whether
it likes it or not, the pendulum always returns to the dead point
fixed by nature. It is of little consequence whether these needs
of nature are called "laws," "ethical norms" or "postulates of
nature." The fact is that they exist; that they have not been invented by man's caprice; that they are really rooted in the nature
which man himself did not fashion; that they are therefore to be
found everywhere; and, consequently, all public law and all law
of nations find in our common nature a clear, solid and durable
foundation.

Security from arbitrary attack

He who would have the star of peace shine out and stand over social life should collaborate toward a complete rehabilitation of the juridical order. . . .

From the juridic order, as willed by God, flows man's inalienable right to juridical security, and by this very fact to a definite sphere of rights, immune from all arbitrary attack. . . .

The State and international community

The idea which credits the State with unlimited authority is not simply an error harmful to the internal life of nations, to their prosperity, and to the larger and well-ordered increase in their well-being, but likewise it injures the relations between peoples, for it breaks the unity of supranational society, robs the law of nations of its foundation and vigor, leads to violation of others' rights and impedes agreement and peaceful intercourse.

Enemy of true union

. . . the human race is bound together by reciprocal ties, moral and juridical, into a great commonwealth directed to the good of all nations and ruled by special laws which protect its unity and promote its prosperity.

Now no one can fail to see how the claim to absolute autonomy for the State stands in open opposition to this natural way that is inherent in man—nay, denies it utterly—and, therefore, leaves the stability of international relations at the mercy of the will of rulers, while it destroys the possibility of true union and fruitful collaboration directed to the general good.

True meaning of sovereignty

In this community of nations, then, every state becomes a part of the system of international law, and hence of natural law, which is both foundation and crown of the whole. Thus the individual nation no longer is—nor in fact was it ever—"sovereign," in the sense of being entirely without restrictions.

"Sovereignty" in the true sense means self-rule and exclusive competence concerning what has to be done and how it is to be done in regard to the affairs of a definite territory, always within the framework of international law, without however becoming dependent on the juridical system of any other state.

Every state is immediately subject to international law. States which would lack this fullness of power, or whose independence of the power of any other state would not be guaranteed by international law, would not be sovereign.

But no state could complain about a limitation of its sovereignty if it were denied the power of acting arbitrarily and without regard for other states. Sovereignty is not a divinization of the state, or omnipotence of the state in the Hegelian sense, or after the manner of absolute juridical positivism.

[V]

Democracy

PARADOXICALLY, despite a flourishing Caesarism and a widespread contempt for personal values, democracy has gained a new foothold in the world, at least within people's hearts. Pius XII himself bears witness to this fact when he asserts "that the people have awakened as it were from a heavy sleep" in assuming a questioning and critical attitude toward those who govern them. "In this psychological atmosphere" says the Pope, "is it any wonder that the tendency toward democracy is capturing the peoples. . ." But this democratic movement will only raise new obstacles for itself if it is not dedicated to a respect for the dignity and rights of others and if there is lacking a consciousness of the responsibility of each to the common good.

In a magnificent discourse, the Pope shows how the concept of democracy is at variance with the notion of a shapeless multitude, "the masses," with which he contrasts the notion of "the people." In contradistinction to the "inert masses," moved from without, "the people" resolves itself into associated persons conscious of their responsibility and their own views, full of exuberant life and self-renewing vigor and possessing a true instinct for the common good.

Against the background of the Papal statements regarding democracy, we can appreciate the importance of the modern Christian democratic movement and the spectacular expansion of Catholic Action. The separation of Church and State in various countries in the circumstances of the time "had for its logical conclusion: leaving the Church to assure by her own means freedom of action, accomplishment of her mission and defense of her rights and liberty" (cf. "The Lay Apostolate—Its Need Today," October 14, 1951, C.M. 50:115, February 1952). Now, as a result of the Christian democratic movement and Catholic Action, the Church's freedom of action will be enhanced; and, moreover, wherever democracy is strong, there will take place an ever more intimate contact between the Church and the individual citizens, thereby benefiting the entire life of society.

R. C. P.

The Incarnation and human dignity

. . . The Church has the mission to announce to the world, which is looking for better and more perfect forms of democracy, the highest and most needed message: the dignity of man, the call to be sons of God. It is the powerful cry, which resounds from the manger of Bethlehem to the furthest confines of the earth at a time when that dignity is tragically low.

The holy story of Christmas proclaims this inviolable dignity of man with a vigor and authority that cannot be gainsaid—an authority and vigor that infinitely transcend all that could be achieved by all other possible declarations of the rights of man. . . .

The democratic form of government

Considering the extent and nature of the sacrifices demanded of all citizens, especially in our day when the activity of the State is so vast and decisive, the democratic form of government appears to many a postulate of nature imposed by reason itself.

The Church and democracy

On this feast day [Christmas] which commemorates both the benignity of the Incarnate Word and the dignity of man, as a person and as a member of society, we direct attention to the problem of democracy. Our aim is to examine the norms by which it should be directed if it is to be a true and healthy democracy—one that answers the needs of the hour. This action shows clearly that the Church is interested and solicitous, not so much about the external structure and organization of a democracy—matters which depend on the particular aspirations of each people—as with its individual citizens. Instead of being the object, merely passive elements, as it were, in the social order, they are in fact, and must continue to be its subject, its foundation, and its end.

Ideal liberty

. . . Of course, democracy aims at putting into practice the ideal of liberty; but the ideal liberty is only that liberty which is far removed from license, that liberty which joins to the consciousness of one's own rights respect for the liberty, dignity and rights of others, and is conscious of one's own responsibility toward the common good. Naturally, this true democracy cannot exist and thrive except in an atmosphere of respect for God and observance of His Commandments, as well as for the Christian solidarity of brotherhood.

Two great rights

Two rights which democracies guarantee to their citizens, as the very term democracy implies, are that they shall have full freedom to set forth their own views of the duties and sacrifices imposed upon them, and that they will not be compelled to obey without being heard.

From the solidarity, harmony and good results produced by this understanding between the citizens and the government, one may decide when a democracy is really healthy and well balanced, and what is its life energy and power of expansion.

The people are awakening

Blessed be the Lord! Out of the mournful groans of sorrow, up from the very depths of the heart-rending anguish of oppressed individuals and countries there arises an aura of hope. To an ever increasing number of noble souls there comes the thought, and with it a clearer, stronger determination, to make this universal upheaval a starting point for a new era of far-reaching renovation— the complete reorganization of the world. . . .

Moreover—this is perhaps the most important point—beneath the sinister lightning of the war that encompasses them, in the blazing heat of the furnace that imprisons them, the peoples have awakened as it were from a heavy sleep. They have taken a new attitude toward the State and toward those who govern—they ask questions, they criticize, and they distrust.

Toward democracy

Taught by bitter experience, they [the people] are more aggressive in opposing the concentration of power in dictatorships that cannot be censured or touched, and in calling for a system of government more in keeping with the dignity and liberty of the citizens. . . .

In this psychological atmosphere, is it any wonder that the tendency toward democracy is capturing the peoples and winning

(65)

a large measure of approval and support from men who hope to play a more efficient part in the destinies of individuals and of society.

The call for democracy and better democracy

When, however, people call for "democracy and better democracy," that demand can have no other meaning than that citizens shall be increasingly placed in a position to hold their own opinions, to voice them, and to make them effective in promoting their general welfare.

Hence follows a first conclusion with its practical consequence. The State is not a distinct entity which mechanically gathers together a shapeless mass of individuals and confines them within a specified territory.

It is and should be in practice the organic and organizing unity of a real people. The people and a shapeless multitude (or as it is called, "the masses") are two distinct concepts.

"The people" and "the masses"

The people lives and moves by its own life energy; the masses are inert of themselves and can only be moved from outside. The people lives by the fullness of life in the men that compose it, each of whom—in his proper place and in his own way—is a person conscious of his own responsibility and of his own views.

The masses, on the contrary, waiting for the impulse from outside, become an easy plaything in the hands of anyone who seeks to exploit their instincts and impressions. They are ready to follow, in turn, today this flag, tomorrow another.

From the exuberant life of a true people, an abundant, rich life

(66)

is diffused in the state and in all its institutions. With a constantly self-renewing vigor, it instills into the citizens the consciousness of their own responsibility, and a true instinct for the common good.

The curtailment of liberty

Whoever would find Our solicitude for true liberty to be without foundation when We speak, as We do, to that part of the world which is generally known as the "free world," should consider that, even there, first real war and then "cold war" forcibly drove social relations toward an inevitable curtailment of liberty itself, while in another part of the world this tendency has reached the ultimate consequences of its development.

Fundamental personal rights

He who would have the star of peace shine out and stand over society should cooperate, for his part, in giving back to the human person the dignity given to it by God from the very beginning. . . .

He should favor, by every lawful means, in every sphere of life, social institutions in which a full personal responsibility is assured and guaranteed. . . . He should uphold respect for and the practical realization of the following fundamental personal rights; the right to maintain and develop one's corporal, intellectual and moral life and especially the right to religious formation and education; the right to worship God in private and public and to carry on religious works of charity; the right to marry and to achieve the aim of married life; the right to conjugal and domestic society; the right to work, as the indispensable means toward the maintenance of family life; the right to free choice of state of life, and hence, too, of the priesthood or religious life; the right to the use of material goods; in keeping with his duties and social limitations.

(67)

Freedom

Freedom, as a basis of normal human relations, cannot be interpreted as an unbridled liberty, whether there is question of individuals or parties, of an entire people, the collectivity as they say today, or even of a totalitarian state, which will use every means, with utter disregard, to make sure of its purpose. No, freedom is something quite different. It is the temple of the moral order erected on harmonious lines; it is the aggregate of the rights and duties of individuals and the family—some of these rights imprescriptible even when an apparent common good might challenge them—of the rights and duties of a nation or state and of the family of nations and states. These rights and duties are carefully measured and balanced by the demands of the dignity of the human person and family on one side, and of the common good on the other.

Individualism

. . . Individual liberty, freed from all bonds and all laws, all objective and social values, is in reality only a death-dealing anarchy. . . .

Elements of true liberty

. . . true liberty . . . is rather a proved disposition for good; it is that self-decision to will what is good and to accomplish it; it is the mastery of one's own faculties, of instincts, of events.

Liberty and the economic order

. . . Genuine and true liberty can only be that of men who feel themselves bound to the objective goal of social economy and enjoy the right to demand that economies be ordered socially so as to guarantee and protect liberty, rather than restrict even in least degree the choice of means to that end. . . .

Positive law and democracy

Positive law can subsist only in so far as it respects the foundations on which human personality rests, as well as the State and the Government. This is the fundamental criterion for determining the health of all forms of government—democracies included. It is the criterion on which the moral value of every particular law should be judged.

[VI]

The World of Labor

A COMPASSION for the multitudes permeates the various Papal utterances having to do with the workers. The Holy Father realizes what the workers have to contend with today in their efforts to improve their lot, for, as he says, they are "opposed by a machinery" which is at variance not only with human nature, but "with God's plan and with the purpose He had in creating the goods of earth." In confronting the workers' problems, the Pope does not deal with them in terms of mere economic or political expediency, but rather from the standpoint of the natural law and Christian ethics. Which means that what he says penetrates to the living conscience of men. Moreover, in offering these guiding principles, he expects that, as with social principles in general, they will be translated into living reality through the combined efforts of men and according to the circumstances, techniques and knowledge of a given society.

In portraying the ideal of the Christian worker, he sees him as reconciling harmoniously the stubborn defense of economic interests with the interests of justice, while purging himself of hatred and looking toward the widest social cooperation.

Especially inspiring are the various Papal remarks on the dignity of working with matter. "Uphold and defend your personal dignity" he exhorts Italian workers, reminding them that they work with matter which has come from the creative hands of God. Again he tells a group of workers that labor is a kind of extension of the creative work of God, thereby making them aware of the great dignity of their creative role as co-workers with Divinity itself.

R. C. P.

New responsibilities

Each social group has an important role to play in the transformation that the world is undergoing, and it is only too clear that the working class in matters that concern it is called today to assume responsibilities that it has never known in the past.

The fundamental fact

Over and above the distinction between employer and employee, which threatens more seriously every day to become a pitiless separation, there is human labor itself: the work to be done, the job to which every man contributes something vital and personal, with a view to supplying society with goods and services adequate to its needs. It lies in the very nature of labor, understood in this sense, to draw men together in a genuine and intimate union, and to restore form and structure to a society which has become shapeless and unstable. This in turn would infuse new life into the relations between society and the state.

A common service

. . . Work unites all men in common service to the needs of the people and in a unified effort toward perfection of self in honor of the Creator and Redeemer. . . .

Basis of unity

. . . Where God is not beginning and end, where the order that
reigns in His creation is not a guide and measure of the freedom
and activity of everyone, unity among men cannot be achieved.
The material conditions of life and labor, taken in themselves, and
resting upon an alleged uniformity of interests, can never form
the basis of the unity of the working class. Would not the attempt
to build on such a foundation amount clearly to an act of violence
against nature, and would it not serve merely to create new op-
pressions and divisions within the human family, at a moment
when every honest laboring man yearns for just and peaceful
organization in private and public economy and over the whole
range of social life?

The road to decadence

. . . social economy is an organizing of workers, and every worker
is endowed with human dignity and freedom. The immoderate
exploitation of genuine human values usually keeps step with that
of nature's treasures, especially of the land, and leads sooner or
later to decadence.

The plight of the worker

. . . But the Church cannot ignore or overlook the fact that the
worker, in his efforts to better his lot, is opposed by a machinery
which is not only not in accordance with his nature, but is at
variance with God's plan and with the purpose He had in creating
the goods of earth.

Trade unions

... Trade unions arose as a spontaneous and necessary consequence of capitalism, established as an economic system. ...

May Our blessing. ...

May Our blessing, in a special way, render ever more efficacious and more perfect your [Christian workers'] "movement." Does not the name itself expressly give this invitation? A movement is not a simple construction, or a purely static organization, no matter how great and how clever it may be. Movement means life; life, the capability of adapting oneself day by day to the duties and activities suggested by various times, places and circumstances; life, gushing forth from the depths, flowing fresh and abundant through the initiative of each individual and group ever on the alert. You may be certain of this: it is precisely this interior source which gives you your true strength rather than the number of your members.

The right to organize

Because social relations is one of man's natural requirements and since it is legitimate to promote by common effort decent livelihood, it is not possible without injustice to deny or to limit either to the producers or to the laboring and farming classes the free faculty of uniting in associations by means of which they may defend their proper rights and secure the betterment of the goods of soul and body, as well as the honest comforts of life. But to unions of this kind, which in past centuries have procured immortal glory for Christianity and for the professions an untarnishable splendor, one cannot everywhere impose an identical discipline and structure which therefore can be varied to meet the different temperament of the people and the diverse circumstances of time.

Christian workers

. . . Your [Italian workers'] ultimate purpose is the formation of authentic Christian workingmen, equally distinguished for skill in the practice of their profession and for fidelity in the practice of their religion; men who are capable of reconciling harmoniously the stubborn defense of their economic interests with the strictest sense of justice, and with the sincere disposition to collaborate with the other classes of society toward Christian reconstruction in every walk of social life (Cf. *Quadragesimo Anno*).

Guiding principles

We are sure that you, Gentlemen [U.S. delegates of the International Labor Organization], will agree that any organization for improving the condition of the working man will be a mechanism without soul and hence without life and fecundity, unless its charter proclaims and effectively prescribes first, respect for the human person in all men, no matter what their social position; secondly, acknowledgment of the solidarity of all people in forming the human family, created by the loving omnipotence of God; thirdly, the imperative demand on society to place the common good above personal gain, the service of each for all.

Religion and the worker

. . . It has been asserted, and continues to be asserted, that religion makes the workman slack and listless in daily life, in the defense of his private and public interests; that it puts him to sleep like opium, keeping him perfectly quiet with the hope of a life in the beyond. What an obvious error! If the Church insists always, in her social doctrine, on the respect due to the inherent dignity of man, if she asks a just salary for the workman in his labor-contract, if she demands that his material and spiritual needs be met by effective assistance, what prompts this teaching if not the fact that the laborer is a human person, that his productive capacity may not be regarded and treated as so much merchandise, that his labor represents always a personal service?

Workers and the national economy

. . . Why should it not be allowable to assign to the workers a just share of responsibility in the establishment and development of the national economy . . . ?

Dignity of working with matter

In every circumstance and on every occasion, dear sons and daughters [Italian workers], uphold and defend your personal dignity. The material with which you work, created by God from the beginning of the world and in the laboratory of ages molded by Him on the earth and deep beneath the surface of the earth by cataclysms, natural evolution, eruptions and transformations so as to prepare the best abode for man and for his work, let that material be for you a continual reminder of the creative hand of God and let it lift your souls to Him, the supreme Lawgiver, whose precepts must be observed even in factory life.

A necessary expression

. . . For work is not only, for every man, a means of decent livelihood, but it is the means through which all those manifold powers

(75)

and faculties with which nature, training and art have endowed the dignity of the human personality, find their necessary expression, and this with a certain natural comeliness. . . .

Human labor and divine creativity

. . . Because it [labor] is productive it continues the work begun by the Creator and represents the full collaboration of each for the benefit of all. . . .

A humble workman

Sublime mystery that He should begin to work before He began to teach: a humble workman before being the teacher of all nations. (Cf. Acts i:1)

Transforming matter

. . . We who, notwithstanding the distance, live always in Our heart among Our children, bent by day and often by night in their indefatigable labor, see you, pottery workers, following with interest every one of the stages in the transformation of the material in your hands and under the action of fire, and each time beholding with affection the results obtained. And that is true for all of you, not only for those among you fashioning and producing such artistic marvels, such graceful forms, designs and metal-like images meant for the healthy and uplifting delight of the eye; but also for those whose industrial products, adapted to domestic use, enhance with harmony and good taste, with the brilliance of their finish, the home for which they are destined.

The nobility of work

... Your [pottery workers'] art, regional and traditional for many centuries, has the noble characteristic of every profession that works the earth. The farmer smears the earth with his sweat and sows seeds that germinate in its breast and furnish men with nutritive bread and delicious fruits. The miner toils to wrest from the earth its most deeply hidden treasures for the benefit of humanity. You work with this earth to transform it from a dark and shapeless mass into something useful, beautiful and brilliant.

A parable for workers

... Jesus, the Divine Master, loved to teach through parables. (Cf. Mark iv:2, 33, 34) He compared our souls to the earth, where he sows the gifts of nature and of grace, which we must make fruitful. We have not the right to let these talents sleep, useless to us and to others; for He will demand an account. He works this earth Himself and teaches us to work it with Him.

He kneads it into the daily vicissitudes of life, and submits it to the fire of trials to make His greatest masterpiece out of the lowliest soul, the one most pitiable in the eyes of man. If in your [pottery] factory the earth could speak, do you think that it would lament the vigor of the hands that fashion it, or that it would complain under the burning caress of fire, which gives it hardness, beauty and splendor?

[VII]

International Community

"AN INTERNATIONAL COMMUNITY is becoming established," says the Pontiff, and, one might add, in a spirit of exultation, since he views this emerging community as the objective manifestation of the essential unity of mankind. Moreover, he points to the message of Bethlehem as its charter, and to the King and Peacemaker as its unseen head. As a result of this widening of communal life, the family itself, the unit of society, has to situate itself in the larger life of mankind, while true patriotism must recognize that the good of each nation is bound up with the good of the entire world.

The Supreme Pontiff compares the institution of a community of nations with the universal mission of the Church, while noting the essential differences. Considering the universal character of the Church, he reminds us that Catholics should be "precisely the people" to live always in that atmosphere of mutual understanding without which common action on the international plane is without substance. Hence "Catholics are saddled with a great responsibility," for they above all "must realize that they are called upon to overcome every vestige of nationalistic narrowness. . . ."

As we see, the Pope has responded with all his authority and with deep humanity to the international community which is taking shape. And he is at pains to show how in this community of nations "every state becomes a part of the system of international law, and hence of natural law. . . . Thus the individual nation no longer is—nor in fact was it ever—'sovereign,' in the sense of being entirely without restrictions."

R. C. P.

International unification advances

International unification is making remarkable strides forward, despite psychological obstacles which are neither easily nor quickly to be overcome. For technology, economics, politics and the needs of a common defense are exerting their pressure, and seem to have the power and the will to achieve their objectives. This very situation imposes a duty on the Church and on Catholics the world over, which requires vigilant attention and serious concern.

A word of hope

. . . There are evident signs which go to show that, in the ferment of all the prejudices and feelings of hate, those inevitable but lamentable offspring of the war psychosis, there is still aflame in the people the consciousness of their intimate mutual dependence for good or for evil, nay, that this consciousness is more alive and active. . . .

A widening of horizons

Although the family is the foundation of all human culture, it must be developed within the collective unity of society. By that are intended all the relations both social and juridical that unite man to his fellowmen and to civil authority. In our own days those relations extend far beyond political frontiers. An international community is becoming established, within which it is essential that each should recognize what place he holds and the duty he must fulfill. This duty is usually defined by enunciating on the one hand the obligations, and on the other the rights and the liberties which the citizen can demand, but which very often remain more or less at the theoretical stage. . . .

A common aim

The Catholic doctrine on the state and civil society has always been based on the principle that in keeping with the will of God, the nations form together a community with a common aim and common duties. Even when the proclamation of this principle and its practical consequences gave rise to violent reactions, the Church denied her assent to the erroneous concept of an absolutely autonomous sovereignty divested of all social obligations.

The Church and universal community

The institution of a community of nations, which today has been partly realized but which is striving to be established and consolidated upon a higher and more perfect level, is an ascent from the lower to the higher, that is, from a plurality of sovereign states to the greatest possible unity.

The Church of Christ has, in virtue of a mandate from her Divine Founder, a similar universal mission. She must draw to herself and bind together in religious unity the men of all races and of all times. But here the process is in a certain sense the contrary: she descends from the higher to the lower.

In the former case, the superior juridical unity of nations was and still is to be created. In the latter, the juridical community with its universal end, its constitution, its powers and those in whom these powers are invested, are already established from the beginning, by the will and decree of Christ Himself. The duty of this universal community from the outset is to incorporate all men and all races (cf. Matt. xxviii:19) and thereby to bring them to the full truth and the grace of Jesus Christ.

The Church, in the fulfillment of this her mission, has always been faced and is still faced in large measure by the same problems which the functioning of a community of sovereign states must overcome; only she feels them more acutely, for she is obligated to the purpose of her mission, determined by her Founder Himself, a purpose which penetrates to the very depths of the spirit and heart of man.

Catholics are extraordinarily well equipped. . . .

Catholics, in the first place, are extraordinarily well equipped to collaborate in the creation of a climate without which a common action on the international plane can have neither substance nor prosperous growth. We mean an atmosphere of mutual understanding, the basic elements of which may be described in terms of mutual respect, or two-way loyalty, which impels people sincerely to accord to others the same rights they claim for themselves; and of a kindly disposition toward the members of other nations, as toward their brothers and sisters.

Catholics and mutual understanding

The Catholics of the whole world should be precisely the people to live always in this atmosphere [of mutual understanding]. They

(81)

are themselves united in the full richness of their Faith—and therefore in what is for man his noblest, most intimate, most controlling interest—no less than in the spreading of that Faith to social and cultural life. Catholics are likewise trained from their childhood to look upon all men, of whatever zone or nation or color, as creatures and images of God, as redeemed by Christ and called to an eternal destiny; to pray for them and to love them. There is no other group of human beings so favorably predisposed, in breadth and in depth, for international understanding.

Responsibility of Catholics

. . . Catholics are saddled with a great responsibility. They above all, that is to say, must realize that they are called upon to overcome every vestige of nationalistic narrowness, and to seek a genuine fraternal encounter of nation with nation.

Faith in a higher community

The conflicts of the past have too often been motivated by a desire to subjugate other nations and to extend the range of one's own power, or by the necessity of defending one's liberty and one's own independent existence.

This time, on the contrary, it is precisely the will to prevent threatening conflicts that urges men toward a supranational juridical community. Utilitarian considerations, which certainly carry considerable weight, point toward the working out of peace.

And finally, perhaps, it is precisely because of technological progress that this mingling of men of different nations has awakened the faith, implanted in the hearts and souls of individuals, in a higher community of men, willed by the Creator and rooted in the unity of their common origin, nature and final destiny.

The community of mankind and the natural law

... [the] advance toward establishing a community of peoples does not look, as to a unique and ultimate norm, to the will of the states, but rather to nature, to the Creator.

The right to existence, the right to respect from others, and to one's good name, the right to one's own culture and national character, the right to develop oneself, the right to demand observance of international treaties and other like rights, are exigencies of the law of nations, dictated by nature itself.

The positive law of different peoples, also indispensable in the community of states, has the office of defining more exactly the rights derived from nature and of adapting them to concrete circumstances, also of making other provisions, directed of course toward the common good, on the basis of a positive agreement which, once freely entered into, has binding force.

An international order

... We insist once again on certain fundamental conditions essential for an international order which will guarantee for all peoples a just and lasting peace and which will be a bountiful source of well-being and prosperity.

[First:] Within the limits of a new order founded on moral principles there is no room for violation of the freedom, integrity and security of other States, no matter what may be their territorial extension or their capacity for defense. . . .

[Secondly:] Within the limits of a new order founded on moral principles there is no place for open or secret oppression of the cultural and linguistic characteristics of national minorities, for the hindrance or restriction of their economic minorities, for the hindrance or restriction of their economic resources, for the limitation or abolition of their natural fertility. . . .

[Thirdly:] Within the limits of a new order founded on moral principles there is no place for that cold and calculating egoism which tends to hoard economic resources and materials destined for the use of all, to such an extent that the nations less favored by nature are not permitted access to them. . . .

[Fourthly:] Within the limits of a new order, founded on moral principles, once the more dangerous principles of armed conflict have been eliminated, there is no place for a total warfare or for a mad rush to armaments. The calamity of a world war, with the economic and social ruin and the moral dissolution and breakdown which follow in its train, cannot be permitted to envelop the human race for a third time. . . .

[Fifthly:] Within the limits of a new order founded on moral principles, there is no place for the persecution of religion and of the Church. . . .

Order within and without

International relations and internal order are intimately related. International equilibrium and harmony depend on the internal equilibrium and development of the individual States in the material, social and intellectual spheres. A firm and steady peace policy toward other nations is, in fact, impossible without a spirit of peace within the nation which inspires trust. It is only, then, by a striving for an integral peace, a peace in both fields, that people will be freed from the cruel nightmare of war, and the material and psychological causes of further discord and disorder will be diminished and gradually eliminated. Every society, worthy of the name, has originated in a desire for peace, and hence aims at attaining peace. . . .

Democracy and the unity of mankind

How far will the representatives and pioneers of democracy be inspired in their deliberations by the conviction that the absolute order of beings and purposes, of which we have repeatedly spoken, comprises also, as a moral necessity and the crown of social development, the unity of mankind and of the family of peoples?

The universal good and the good of each

. . . in working for the good of all, each of you [Catholic women] will work for the welfare of her own country and the welfare of her family—precisely because order is one: it cannot prevail in individuals, in nations, in the whole of humanity, unless everything is in its place; unless God, therefore, occupies everywhere the only place that is properly His due: the first. . . .

Serving country and mankind

Each one of you [members of Foreign Press Association] has the wish to serve his country. But serve it with the conviction that its good relations with other states, an understanding of their character and respect for their rights belong also to the common good and welfare of the people of one's own country, and that these are amongst the most effective means for the preparation and consolidation of peace. The war and postwar—in spite of their horrors and their miseries—had this much of good in them, that they made men much more aware of this fact.

The nations and world community

In the light of this unity of all mankind, which exists in law and in fact, individuals do not feel themselves isolated units, like grains of sand, but united by the very force of their nature and by their eternal destiny, into an organic, harmonious mutual relationship which varies with the changing of times.

And the nations, despite a difference of development due to diverse conditions of life and of culture, are not destined to break the unity of the human race, but rather to enrich and embellish it by the sharing of their own peculiar gifts and by that reciprocal interchange of goods which can be possible and efficacious only when a mutual love and a lively sense of charity unite all the sons of the same Father and all those redeemed by the same Divine Blood.

The nations and international law

In this community of nations, then, every state becomes a part of the system of international law, and hence of natural law, which is both foundation and crown of the whole. Thus the individual nation no longer is—nor in fact was it ever—"sovereign," in the sense of being entirely without restrictions.

No artificial uniformity

Just as, therefore, if it is to be true to the spirit of federalism, the future world political organization cannot under any pretext allow itself to be caught up in the play of artificial uniformity, so also it will enjoy effective authority only insofar as it safeguards and encourages everywhere the life that is proper to a healthy human community, to a society in which all the members cooperate together for the well-being of the whole of humanity.

The unseen head

. . . To the millions who are disposed to become members of this world alliance [a community of nations], the charter of which is the message of Bethlehem and its unseen head, the King and Peacemaker who lies before us in the manger, We direct at this juncture our heartfelt appeal.

From Bethlehem to Golgotha

... It is in the days of trial, rather than in untroubled hours, that men of all nations should realize that they are brothers. The real meaning, the lofty mission and the power to reconcile of this brotherhood has never been, nor shall ever be extolled with such force as it was by "the first-born among many brethren" (*Rom.* viii:29), Who from Bethlehem to Golgotha preached by His example more than by His words that great and universal brotherhood of men.

The discovery of brotherhood

But is it really necessary that men reach the threshold of death in order to discover that they are brothers? This belated charity is to be admired, but is not enough. The Christian peoples must become conscious of the brotherly ties that bind them to each other, and their souls must find the strength, sometimes a truly heroic one, to pardon each other, without which it will never be possible to attain true and permanent concord.

True brotherhood

... salvation will not come for the world until mankind, deriving its inspiration from the teachings and example of Christ, comes to recognize that all men are children of the one Father Who is in Heaven, destined to be truly brothers through union with His Divine Son, whom He sent to be Redeemer of all.

(87)

Only this brotherhood gives to man, with the highest sense of personal dignity, assurance of true equality, the necessary basis of justice.

Only this brotherhood guarantees the gift of true liberty in the enjoyment of our rights and in the fulfillment of our duties in obedience to the laws given by Almighty God and His Divine Son for the morality and sanctity of human life.

Only this brotherhood inspires, nourishes and revives in the hearts of men that true charity which abhors all oppression and violence; which rises above egoism, whether in individuals or peoples; which is able to sacrifice itself for the common good and to give generously of itself to the destitute and to relieve those who are suffering. . . .

The longing for larger groupings

. . . the idea of a United Europe, the Council of Europe and other movements of the kind are a manifestation of the world's need to break through, or at least to make more flexible, politically and economically, the old rigid lines of geographical frontiers, and to form larger groupings between countries with a view to common life and action. . . .

Away with barriers!

Away with the barriers! Break down the barbed-wire fences! Let each people be free to know the life of other peoples; let that segregation of some countries from the rest of the civilized world, so dangerous to the cause of peace, be abolished. How earnestly the Church desires to smooth the way for these friendly relations among peoples. For her East and West do not represent opposite ideals but share a common heritage, to which both have generously contributed and to which both are called to contribute in the future also. By virtue of her divine mission she is a mother to all peoples, and a faithful ally and wise guide to all who seek peace.

Prayers for the United Nations

. . . If ever an assembly of men, gathered at a critical cross-road in history, needed the help of prayer, it is this assembly of the United Nations.

Hence We ask you, venerable brothers, you, Our cherished sons in the sacred priesthood and you, Our beloved children in Christ Jesus, to pray. Let Our voice carry beyond you to all your fellow Catholics in America, yes to all Catholics in every country on the face of the earth. And We like to hope that you will be joined by all men of good will. . . .

Support for the agencies and offices of the United Nations

. . . We are happy to assure all the agencies and offices of the United Nations, destined to bring international assistance to the working man, that the Church is ever prepared to support their efforts with her most sympathetic collaboration.

Public opinion

When there is question of relations between nations and states, the educating of public opinion to look at things as they are and to consider truth dispassionately, with calm and dignity, is one of the essential conditions for the smoothing down of opposition, for bringing peoples together and for peace.

[VIII]

Cultural Diversity

PIUS XII has often insisted on respect for the wholesome traditions, aspirations and cultures of the various peoples. He is dead against an artificial uniformity, a "mechanical unitarism," which would discourage everywhere the life that is proper to the various communities. In stressing the need for a true organic unity which will achieve unity in diversity, the Pope has behind him the long and rich experience of the Church in facing extreme cultural diversity and building upon it. With St. Augustine, he proclaims the fact that the Church is "not anxious about diversities in customs, laws, institutions; she does not cut off or destroy any of these but preserves and observes them." And with almost 2000 years of the Church's experience to point the way, men must go about the business of building an international community on the foundation of respect for "the wholesome cultural peculiarities of the sundry peoples of the world."

R. C. P.

A guiding principle

The Church, from the beginning down to our own time, has always followed this wise practice: let not the Gospel on being introduced into any new land destroy or extinguish whatever its people possess that is naturally good, just or beautiful. For the Church, when she calls people to a higher culture and a better way of life, under the inspiration of the Christian religion, does not act like one who recklessly cuts down and uproots a thriving forest. No, she grafts a good scion upon the wild stock that it may bear a crop of more delicious fruit.

Divine Wisdom

The Church of Christ, the faithful depository of the teaching of Divine Wisdom, cannot and does not think of deprecating or disdaining the particular characteristics which each people, with jealous and intelligible pride, cherishes and retains as a precious heritage. Her aim is a supernatural union in all-embracing love, deeply felt and practiced, and not the unity which is exclusively external and superficial and by that very fact weak.

The Church hails with joy and follows with her maternal blessing every method of guidance and care which aims at a wise and orderly evolution of particular forces and tendencies having their origin in the individual character of each race, provided that they are not opposed to the duties incumbent on men from their unity of origin and common destiny. She has repeatedly shown in her missionary enterprises that such a principle of action is the guiding star of her universal apostolate. Pioneer research and investigation, involving sacrifice, devotedness and love on the part of her missionaries of every age, have been undertaken in order to facilitate the deeper appreciative insight into the most varied civilizations and to put their spiritual values to account for a living and vital preaching of the Gospel of Christ. . . .

"Not anxious about diversities"

. . . ever more fully is verified in the Church of today that phenomenon which St. Augustine praised in his *City of God:* the Church, he wrote, "recruits her citizens from all nations, and in every language assembles her community of pilgrims on earth; she is not anxious about diversities in customs, laws, institutions; she does not cut off or destroy any of these, but rather preserves and observes them. Even the differences in different nations she directs to the one common end of peace on earth, as long as they do not impede the worship of the one, supreme, and true God."

Gladly welcomes them

As you well know, the Catholic religion, far from being opposed to true doctrine or to those institutions of public or private life that are founded on justice, freedom, and charity, on the contrary, furthers, sustains and perfects them. It does not despise or reject the characteristic genius of various peoples, their particular customs, or art or civilization, but, instead, readily accepts them and, one may say, gladly welcomes them as a new and varied adornment of its own culture.

A universal experience

For the Church with her mission has been, and is, confronted with men and nations of marvelous culture, with others of almost incredible lack of civilization, and with all possible intermediate degrees: diversity of extraction, of language, of philosophy, of religious belief, of national aspirations and characteristics; free peoples and enslaved peoples; peoples that have never belonged to the Church and peoples that have been separated from her communion.

Mutual esteem

. . . Briefly, the guarantee of the future demands [among other things] *Mutual esteem* in a double sense: not scorning a nation because, for example, it appears less gifted than one's own. Such scorn would denote a narrow mental outlook. The comparison of national aptitudes must embrace the broadest fields. The attempt to make such a comparison requires deep knowledge and long experience. Furthermore, it is necessary to respect the right of each people to carry on its own activities. This right cannot be artificially restricted or strangled by restraining measures.

Versus a narrow mental outlook

We have noted on another occasion how necessary it is—if every mutual overture is not to be poisoned—to maintain a respectful reserve and regard for the wholesome cultural peculiarities of the sundry peoples of the world. . . .

The right to one's own culture

The right to existence, the right to respect from others and to one's good name, the right to one's own culture and national character, the right to develop oneself, the right to demand observance of international treaties, and other like rights, are exigencies of the law of nations, dictated by nature itself.

Respecting inborn inclinations

The jurist, the statesman, the individual state, as well as the community of states should . . . take account of all the inborn inclinations of individuals and communities in their contracts and reciprocal relations. . . .

No mechanical unitarism

You [members of World Mov't for World Federal Gov't] are of the opinion that this world political organization, in order to be effective, must be federal in form. If by this you understand that it should not be enmeshed in a mechanical unitarism, again you are in harmony with the principles of social and political life so firmly founded and sustained by the Church. . . .

Just as, therefore, if it is to be true to the spirit of federalism, the future world political organization cannot under any pretext allow itself to be caught up in the play of mechanical unitarism, so also it will enjoy effective authority only insofar as it safeguards and encourages everywhere the life that is proper to a healthy human community, to a society in which all the members cooperate together for the well-being of the whole of humanity.

The profound experience of a people

. . . In a society that ignores its healthiest and most fertile traditions, folklore strives to make it maintain a living continuity with the past; not a continuity imposed by outside forces, but one resulting from the profound feelings of generations, which have found in folklore the expression of their special aspirations, their beliefs, desires, and sorrows, their glorious memories of the past and their hopes for the future. . . . But it must not be forgotten that in Christian countries, or in those which once were Christian, religious faith and the people's lives formed a unity comparable to the unity of soul and body. Today, where such a unity is lacking or where faith has become weak, can popular traditions, deprived of their vital principles, be maintained or renewed even artificially? In regions where such unity is still preserved folklore is not merely a curious survival from past ages; it is a manifestation of present-day life, which recognizes its debt to the past and attempts to maintain itself and adapt itself intelligently to new situations.

[IX]

Peace

UNIVERSALLY ACCLAIMED the Apostle of Peace, Pius XII has taught us by example what the "Christian will to peace" signifies, and he has made it easier for us to respond deeply to those stirring words, "Blessed be the peacemaker." Peace, he declares, "is the fairest of all God's gifts." It is "desired by all upright men," and is "the fruit of love and justice." To serve the cause of peace is, among other things, to "lift men's minds to heaven and to snatch them from the power of Satan" and "to fulfill the sovereign law of God," a law of bountiful goodness and love.

Even when he points to the spiritual anemia of nations as a threat to peace, the Pope can yet single out what is so promising in the world today, namely, the widening participation of the people in the cause of peace. And there is great need for such participation, for appalling destruction faces the world unless a peace is achieved which will once and for all banish the threat of ABC warfare, atomic, biological and chemical. The Pope's graphic description of the horrors that confront us is well worth reading over and over again. "When will it come about" he asks, "that the learned ones of the world will turn the wonderful discovery of the profound forces of matter exclusively to purposes of peace . . . ?"

R. C. P.

"War on war"

If a generation has ever had to appreciate in the depths of its conscience the call: "War on war," it is certainly the present generation.

It has passed through an ocean of blood and tears wider and deeper than mankind has ever before encountered. It has lived through indescribable atrocities so intensely that the recollection of their horrors must remain stamped in its memory and even in the deepest recesses of its soul as the picture of a hell against which anyone who cherishes a sense of humanity desires more than anything else to close the door forever.

A growing multitude

One thing that has contributed significantly toward making men open their hearts to the hope of this fair and more peaceful morrow is the fact that, while the instruments of destruction have reached a potency never before known, and while the world finds itself on the eve of still more dramatic and, according to some, decisive events, the discussion of the fundamental outlook and of the detailed guiding principles of the future peace attracts more and more participants; the numbers and the interest of those joining in that discussion grow from hour to hour.

The cause of peace

. . . To serve the cause of peace is to serve justice. To serve the cause of peace is to serve the interests of the people, especially the

(97)

lowly and dispossessed. To serve the cause of peace is to face the future with serene and unruffled countenance. To serve the cause of peace is to hasten the day when all nations without exception shall lay aside their rivalries and feuds, and embrace one another as brothers. To serve the cause of peace is to save civilization. To serve the cause of peace is to preserve the human family from new and unutterable misfortunes; it is to lift men's minds to heaven and to snatch them from the power of Satan. To serve the cause of peace is to fulfill the sovereign law of God, which is a law of bountiful goodness and love.

The Christian will for peace

The Christian will for peace is easily identified. Obedient to the divine precept of peace, it will never turn a question of national prestige or honor into an argument for war or even for a threat of war. It is very careful to avoid recourse to the force of arms in the defense of rights which, however legitimate, do not offset the risk of kindling a blaze with all its tremendous spiritual and material consequences.

Always room for a peaceful settlement

For those who see things in the light of the supernatural, there is no doubt that even in the most serious conflicts of human and national interest there is always room for a peaceful settlement. . . .

The work for peace

. . . the Holy See's work in favor of peace and international concord . . . seems to be as thorny as it is difficult. It is so difficult, because the fundamental conceptions of justice and love, which make for individual happiness and the nobility of common social life, have in many respects fallen into oblivion or contempt by a false process of thought and action which humanizes what is divine and divinizes what is human.

Spiritual anemia

If the desire to prevent war is to be truly efficacious, above all a remedy must be sought for the spiritual anemia of nations, for the ignorance of individual responsibility before God and man, and for the want of a Christian order which alone is able to guarantee peace. To this goal the resources of the Church are now directed.

A dreadful future threatens

. . . if in the heavens all is peace and joy, on earth the reality is quite otherwise. Here, in place of the serene joy whose secret was revealed by Christ Himself, there is year by year a mounting anxiety and, one might say, trepidation on the part of the peoples of the world by reason of their fear of a third world conflict and of a dreadful future, placed at the mercy of new destructive arms of unprecedented violence.

These means of destruction—as We had already occasion to state and to fear as far back as February, 1943—are capable of bringing about "a dangerous catastrophe for our entire planet" (*Acta Apostolicae Sedis* 1943, Page 75), of causing the total extermination of all animal and vegetable life and of all the works of man over vaster regions; and they are now capable, with artificially radioactive isotopes of extended average life, of polluting in a lasting manner the atmosphere, the land and also the oceans, even where these areas are very distant from the zones directly stricken and contaminated by the nuclear explosions.

Gigantic destruction

. . . before the eyes of a terrified world there is presented a preview of gigantic destruction, of extensive territories rendered uninhabitable and unfit for human use over and above the biological consequence that can result, either by the changes brought about by germs and microorganisms, or through the uncertain effect which a prolonged radioactive stimulus can have upon greater organisms, including man, and upon their future offspring.

Pathogenic mutations

. . . We do not wish to omit a reference to the danger that could result for future generations from mutagenic intervention, obtainable or perhaps already obtained by new means, for the purpose of deviating the patrimony of man's hereditary factors from their natural development; and this also for the reason that among such deviations there probably are not lacking, or would not be lacking, those pathogenic mutations which are the causes of transmittable diseases and monstrosities.

Banishment of ABC warfare

For Our part, We will tirelessly endeavor to bring about, by means of international agreements—always in subordination to the principle of legitimate self-defense (cf. however, *Acta Apostolicae Sedis*, 1953, pp. 748-49)—the effective proscription and banishment of atomic, biological and chemical warfare (*ibid.*, p. 749).

Serving peace

When will it come about that the learned ones of the world will turn the wonderful discovery of the profound forces of matter exclusively to purposes of peace: to enable man's activity to produce energy at a low cost which would alleviate the scarcity and correct the unequal geographical distribution of the sources of wealth and work, as also to offer new arms to medicine and agriculture, and to peoples new fountains of prosperity and well-being?

Fairest of all God's gifts

. . . We speak of that peace which Our predecessor of beloved memory so earnestly besought from God, offering indeed his own life, for the harmonious reconciliation of men; peace, the fairest of all God's gifts, that passes all understanding, the peace that all men of feeling cannot but strive for; the peace, in fine, which arises from justice and charity. This is the peace to which We exhort all, the peace which brings new warmth to those already joined in friendship with God, which moderates and tempers private interests with the sacred love of Jesus Christ, the peace which joins nations and peoples through mutual brotherly love, so that each race, by a feeling common to all, by friendly helping alliances, strives, with God's inspiration and aid, for the greater happiness of the whole human family.

A real peace

. . . a real peace in conformity with the dignity of man and the Christian conscience can never be a harsh imposition supported by arms, but rather is the result of a provident justice and a responsible sense of equity toward all.

Justice—a condition of peace

. . . Briefly, the guarantee of the future demands: [among other things] 1. Justice, which applies an equal standard to both sides.

That which a nation or a state demands for itself with an elementary sense of right, that which it would never renounce, must be conceded without conditions to the other nation and to the other state. Is that not obvious? Yes, but national pride is too inclined, almost unconsciously, to apply two standards. It is necessary to use intelligence and will in order to remain objective in the difficult area where national interests are discussed.

Peace, a moral and juridical process

. . . A true peace is not the mathematical result of a proportion of forces, but in its last and deepest meaning is a moral and juridical process. It is not, in fact, achieved without the employment of force, and its very existence needs the support of a normal measure of power.

But the real function of this force, if it is to be morally correct, should consist in protecting and defending, and not in lessening or suppressing rights. . . .

To renew the face of the earth

No, Venerable Brethren, safety does not come to peoples from external means, from the sword, which can impose conditions of peace but does not create peace. Forces that are to renew the face of the earth should proceed from within, from the spirit.

A fervent wish

. . . May the United Nations Organization become the full and faultless expression of this international solidarity for peace, erasing from its institutions and its statutes every vestige of its original which was of necessity a solidarity in war.

Confidence in the international community

. . . We are confident that the international community can banish every danger of war and establish the peace, and, as far as the Church is concerned, can guarantee to her freedom of action everywhere. . . .

A fundamental postulate

A fundamental postulate of any just and honorable peace is an assurance for all nations great or small, powerful or weak, of their right to life and independence. The will of one nation to live must never mean the sentence of death passed upon another. When this equality of rights has been destroyed, attacked, or threatened, order demands that reparation shall be made, and the measure and extent of that reparation is determined, not by the sword nor by the arbitrary decision of self-interest, but by the rules of justice and reciprocal equity.

Mass psychosis

We have often insisted that responsibility [for the fearful state of things at the present] be attributed, as far as possible, to those who are guilty, but they must be justly and clearly distinguished from the people as a whole. We have to admit that both sides have been affected by mass psychosis. It is very difficult for the individual to escape from it, and not to let his freedom be diminished by it. Those who have suffered great calamities from the mass psychosis of another nation should always ask themselves whether that nation, in the depth of its heart, was not roused to fury by the evil-doers of their own nation. The hatred of nations is always a cruel injustice, absurd and unworthy of man. . . .

[X]

Science

Pius xii has been most effective in dispelling the misconceptions which have gathered around the relation between religion and science, misconceptions nursed along by those who have failed to comprehend the historical complexities in this matter. We have but to peruse the statements in this section to grasp the true mind of the Church in regard to science. And enough is said to make us realize, what many scholars now tell us, that so far from being unfriendly to science, the Church instilled in man attitudes which rendered its development inevitable. Reading through these excerpts from Papal documents, one is overwhelmed by the force of the Pope's appreciation of the sciences and his whole positive approach. One notes a fine poetic sensibility which gives an added power to all that he says—a poetic sensibility which is so necessary if we are to grasp imaginatively the immensity of scientific achievement and its importance in human destiny.

R. C. P.

Traces of the Divine Intelligence

. . . She [The Church] has, indeed, good reason to know that every truth, every new scientific discovery, must be welcomed as one more trace, as it were, of the Divine Intelligence and one more token of the power of God.

The conquests of science

. . . We have no need to show how We understand and highly esteem the activities and conquests of the natural sciences and of technology. . . .

Along new roads

The admirable conquest by the human intellect which taxes and investigates the laws of nature is carrying humanity with it along new roads.

Truth not opposed to truth

Whatever new truth the sincere human mind is able to find certainly cannot be opposed to truth already acquired, since God, the Highest Truth, has created and guides human intellect, not that it may daily oppose new truths to rightly established ones but rather that, having eliminated errors which may have crept in, it may build truth upon truth in the same order and structure that exist in reality, the source of truth.

Our Masters

We are not creators: we create neither the world nor truth. They are the standards to which our minds must conform. Nature stands between God and ourselves, and truth is inseparable from nature. God, nature, and truth, those are our Masters; we are their humble servants, pilgrims to God through nature and truth, the agents of a joyous adventure. Your task is to know and to increase humanity's treasures of knowledge. It is a work of love, not of dissension, akin to the work of the Church, which throughout the centuries has proved to be the mother of science and progress.

A humiliating servitude

. . . the science which has apostatized from the life of the spirit, while it deluded itself into thinking that it has acquired full liberty and autonomy in denying God, finds itself today punished by a servitude more humiliating than ever before. For it has become the slave and the almost blind follower of policies and orders which take no account of the rights of truth or of the human person. . . .

Man learns from two books. . . .

Man learns from two books: the universe, for the human study of the things created by God; and the Bible, for the study of God's superior will and truth. One belongs to reason, the other to faith. Between them there is no clash. Faith is not tyrannical; it is a free act; it respects reason, though it leads it but gently. And as faith is the friend of reason, so the Church is a friend to science. She respects its freedom, its methods and principles, merely intervening to save it from errors against the faith.

Facts and their interpretation

The distinction between sure facts and their interpretation is as fundamental to the researcher as the definition of truth. A fact is always true because it can contain no ontological error. But the same thing is not true of scientific development. Here one runs the danger of coming to premature conclusions or of committing errors of judgment.

All this breeds respect for facts and for the unity of facts, prudence in the expression of scientific propositions, sobriety in scientific judgments, and modesty, which is so greatly appreciated among scholars and which instills a consciousness of the limits of human knowledge. All this favors the openness of the mind and the submissiveness of the true man of science, who is far removed from holding on to his ideas when they are not sufficiently grounded. Finally, this leads to an unprejudiced examination and judgment of the opinion of others.

When a man is of this disposition of mind, respect for truth goes quite naturally hand in hand with truthfulness, that is to say, the agreement between personal convictions and scientific opinions expressed orally or in writing.

No barriers to truth

If you reflect on what We have said about research and scientific knowledge, you will understand that neither from the point of view of reason nor from the point of view of Christian thought can barriers be placed in the way of research, knowledge or the affirmation of truth. There are barriers, but they do not imprison truth. They aim at keeping unproven hypotheses from being considered as established facts, at keeping men from forgetting the necessity of complementing one source of knowledge by another, and at checking the erroneous interpretation of the scale of values and the degree of certainty of a source of knowledge. It is to avoid these causes of error that barriers exist; but there are no barriers to truth.

The act of knowing

The wise men of old were already astonished, and rightly so, at the inventive power of the human mind. Even more in our days do we admire the perfecting and unceasing adaptation of the methods man uses in order to know the world in which he lives. Now the act of knowing consists essentially in bringing the multiplicity of reality to the unity of the mind, in discovering in the complexity of data the permanent elements which explain them and account for their ordering and then in explaining according to synthetic formulas the laws which govern reality. The domain of the natural sciences, wherein reigns the determinism of matter, offers an appropriate field for such intellectual activity and lends itself relatively easily to the elaboration of precise laws.

The conquest of cosmic space

Although We are conscious that We are addressing distinguished scholars [World Astronomical Congress] who are more conversant with science than We are, still We cannot refrain from recalling at least the chief steps in the wonderful progress achieved by astronomy and astrophysics in the last fifty years, pointing out the milestones which are at the same time so important for more exalted considerations.

That which was an enigma and a dream for the astronomers of the past, and which has become for contemporary astronomers a brilliant reality surpassing every expectation, may perhaps be well expressed in these words: the conquest of cosmic space.

Observation, intelligence, new technical means have placed in the hands of astronomical science something like a gigantic compass which scientists have daily extended further and further in the universe, until the radius now attained far surpasses the hitherto foreseeable dimensions.

How many barriers, erected especially by enormous distances, have been thrust aside during the last decades through the invincible and never satisfied spirit of research on the part of scientists.

Mastering the immense universe

Though man is essentially bound within the narrow limits of bodily conditions, he has exceeded every expectation that the limited power of the human senses at first could promise him, and with his intelligence has succeeded in mastering the immense universe.

A wonderful climb to the heavens

Truly extraordinary has man's labor been if one considers the starting point of his wonderful climb to the heavens; for the senses, from whose data man necessarily has to start, dispose of a very limited power of knowing, generally restricted to their immediate neighborhood in space and time.

The first accomplishment of the human spirit, therefore, consists in having broken down the narrow enclosure imposed on the senses by the conditions of their very nature. It has done this by inventing means and constructing ingenious instruments which increase beyond all limits both the amplitude and the precision of sense perceptions. . . .

While the human spirit thus gradually increases the power of the senses, it uses these heightened potentialities in order to deepen its researches on nature, thinking up a thousand devices for revealing the most subtle and abstruse phenomena.

The deep interior of the solar orb

Not even the deep interior of the solar orb escapes the penetrating gaze of the human mind equipped with astrophysical theories; the intelligence of man thus succeeds in following the transformation of matter itself, practically witnessing the nuclear processes which take place in the center of the sun and which compensate for the energy losses due to the escape of solar radiation during billions of years.

Bold and unafraid

Bold and unafraid, the human spirit does not hesitate even before the tremendous cataclysms occurring in a nova or supernova, but measures the immense velocities of the exploding gases and tries to discover the causes of the observed phenomena.

It even retraces the path of the fleeing galaxies back through the billions of years of past time, in order to witness the mighty cosmic processes that took place in the first morning of the creation of the world.

The spirit of infinitesimal man

What thing is then this spirit of infinitesimal man, physically lost on the ocean of the universe but daring to ask his extremely limited senses to discover the countenance and the history of the boundless universe, and then succeeding in revealing both of them?

Only one answer, strikingly evident, can be given, and that is: The spirit of man belongs to an order of being essentially different from, and superior to, that of matter, even though that matter be of immeasurable mass.

Finally, this question spontaneously presents itself: Will this path, begun by the spirit of man with undisputed honor to himself, be open indefinitely to him in the future, and will it be trod by him unceasingly until he is able to reveal the very last mystery of the universe?

Or, on the contrary, is the mystery of nature so stupendous and so hidden that the human spirit, through its own intrinsic limitations and inadequacies, will never succeed in fathoming it completely?

The answer of vigorous minds who have penetrated most deeply into the secrets of the cosmos is quite modest and reserved: We are, they think, at the very beginning; there is a long way still to go and the path will be tirelessly followed; however, it is completely improbable that even the most gifted investigator will ever succeed in recognizing, and much less in solving, the mysteries locked up in the physical universe.

The meeting of spirit and Spirit

Both happy and transcendent is this meeting of the human spirit and the Spirit of the Creator [in scientific discovery]. We mean a spirit truly divine and not a world soul to be confounded with the universe, as pantheism dreamed of.

An unspeakable harmony

. . . by your [members of Pontifical Academy of Science] research, your unveiling of the secrets of nature and your teaching of men to direct the forces of nature toward their own welfare, you preach at the same time, in the language of figures, formulae and discoveries, the unspeakable harmony of the work of an all-wise God.

In fact, according to the measure of its progress, and contrary to affirmations advanced in the past, true science discovers God in an ever-increasing degree—as though God were waiting behind every door opened by science. We would even say that from this progressive discovery of God, which is realized in the increase of knowledge, there flow benefits not only for the scientist himself when he reflects as a philosopher—and how can he escape such reflection?—but also for those who share in these new discoveries or make them the object of their own considerations.

Illustrations in the midst of shadows

Genuine philosophers profit from these discoveries [of science] in a very special way, because when they take these scientific conquests as the basis for their rational speculations, their conclusions thereby acquire greater certainty, while they are provided with clearer illustrations in the midst of possible shadows, and more convincing assistance in establishing an ever more satisfying response to difficulties and objections.

Philosophical arguments

Thus stimulated and guided [by scientific discoveries], the human intellect approaches that demonstration of the existence of God which Christian wisdom recognizes in those philosophical arguments which have been carefully examined throughout the centuries by giants in the world of knowledge, and which are already well known to you in the presentation of the "five ways" which the Angelic Doctor, St. Thomas, offers as a speedy and safe road to lead the mind to God. We have called these arguments "philosophical." This does not mean that they are *a prioristic,* as they are accused of being by a narrow-minded and incoherent Positivism. Even though they draw their demonstrative force from the power of human reason, they are nevertheless based on concrete realities established by the senses and by science.

Vestiges of God

. . . if the primitive experience of the ancients could provide human reason with sufficient arguments to demonstrate the existence of God, then with the expanding and deepening of the field of human experiments, the vestiges of the Eternal One are discernible in the visible world in ever more striking and clearer light. . . .

The presence of God

. . . Has there ever been a time until now when the presence of God has manifested itself so forcefully—We were almost about to say, so visibly—to human reason as at the present? The natural sciences are making astonishing progress and each one of their discoveries prompts man to exclaim: "Here is the hand of a Creator!"

Inexhaustible riches

The scholar who devotes himself to labors such as yours [radiology], does not serve an idol, but in trying to know the inexhaustible riches of physical and living nature, he discloses a bit more every day the treasures placed by the Creator in His handiwork. He is like one who discovers new lands for the glory of his Lord. . . .

No reason to be fearful

It is . . . helpful to consider . . . if and to what degree these proofs [of God's existence] have been weakened, as is not infrequently affirmed, by the fact that modern physics has formulated new basic principles, ruled out or modified certain ancient ideas, whose content was perhaps judged in the past to be fixed and definitive, such as time, space, motion, causality, substance—all of which concepts are supremely important for the question which now occupies us.

The question, then, is not one of revising the philosophical proofs, but rather of inquiring into the physical foundations from which they flow although limitations of time will oblige Us to restrict Our attention to only some few of these foundations. There is no reason to be fearful of surprises. Not even science itself aims to go outside that world which today, as yesterday, presents itself through these "five modes of being," whence the philosophical demonstration of the existence of God proceeds and draws its force.

Mutability and the teleological order

From these "modes of being" of the world around us which, in greater or less degrees of comprehension, are noted with equal evidence by both the philosopher and the human mind in general, there are two which modern science has, in a marvelous degree, fathomed, verified and deepened beyond all expectations: 1) *the mutability of things, including their origin and their end;* and 2) *the teleological order which stands out in every corner of the cosmos.* The contribution thus made by science to the two philosophical arguments which hinge on these facts, and which constitute the first and the fifth ways of St. Thomas, is most notable.

The deepest recesses of nature

To the first way [first proof for God's existence] physics, especially, has provided an inexhaustible mine of experiments, revealing the fact of mutability in the deepest recesses of nature, where previously no human mind could ever even suspect its existence and vastness. Thus physics has provided a multiplicity of empirical facts which are of tremendous assistance to philosophical reasoning. We say "assistance," because the very direction of these same transformations, precisely in view of the certainty afforded by physics, seems to Us to surpass the value of a mere confirmation and acquires almost the structure and dignity of a physical argument which is in great part new and more acceptable, persuasive and welcome to many minds.

A vision of unity

With similar richness other sciences, especially the astronomical and the biological sciences, have in our own day contributed to the argument from order [for God's existence] such a vast array of knowledge, and so to speak, so stupefying a vision of the conceptual unity animating the cosmos, and of the teleology directing its movements, as to anticipate for modern man the joy which the Poet imagines in the empyrean heaven when he beheld in God "In one volume bound by love, the same that the universe holds scattered through its maze" (Dante, *Paradiso*, Canto 33, 85-7).

Priceless services

Wishing to give here only a rapid summary of the priceless services rendered by modern science to the demonstration of the existence of God, We shall limit Ourselves, first of all, to the fact of changes, pointing out principally their amplitude and vastness and, so to speak, their totality which modern physics meets in the inanimate cosmos. . . .

"Everything is in flux"

At first sight it is rightly a source of wonderment to recognize how the knowledge of the fact of mutability has gained ever greater ground, both in the macrocosm and in the microcosm, according as science has made new progress, as though confirming with new proofs the theory of Heraclitus: "everything is in flux": *panta rhei.* . . .

The world bespeaks a Creator

The growing knowledge of the periodic system of chemical elements, the discovery of the corpuscular irradiations of radio-active substances, our knowledge of cosmic rays and of the loss of the atom's free energy in the electron rings and the nucleus—all this, and much more besides, demonstrates, with a clarity hard to surpass, the mutability of the cosmos, of the universe as such, even down to the sub-atomic energies of the atom's nucleus. The world is marked with the imprint of mutability, of a beginning and an end in time; and with cogent and irresistible voice it be-speaks a Creator, completely distinct from the world itself, and by His very nature immutable. We were not surprised to read, therefore, that recently a great non-Catholic scientist, Max Planck, shortly before dying declared that the physical world led him to recognize the existence of a personal God.

The scientist of today. . . .

. . . the scientist of today, directing his gaze more deeply into the heart of nature than his predecessor of a hundred years ago, knows well that inorganic matter is, so to speak, in its innermost being, countersigned with the stamp of mutability and that, consequently, its existence and its subsistence demand a reality entirely different and one which is by its very nature invariable.

Let there be light

It is undeniable that when a mind enlightened and enriched with modern scientific knowledge weighs this problem [the state and quality of original matter] calmly, it feels drawn to break through the circle of completely independent or autochthonous matter, whether uncreated or self-created, and to ascend to a creating Spirit. With the same clear and critical look with which it examines and passes judgment on facts, it perceives and recognizes the work of creative omnipotence, whose power, set in motion by the mighty "Fiat" pronounced billions of years ago by the Creating Spirit, spread out over the universe, calling into existence, with a gesture of generous love, matter bursting with energy. In fact, it would seem that present-day science, with one sweeping step back across millions of centuries, has succeeded in bearing witness to that primordial "Fiat lux" uttered at the moment when, along with matter, there burst forth from nothing a sea of light and radiation, while the particles of chemical elements split and formed into millions of galaxies.

Science's contribution

What, then, is the importance of modern science for the argument for the existence of God based on the mutability of the cosmos? By means of exact and detailed research into the macrocosm and the microcosm, it has considerably broadened and deepened the empirical foundation on which this argument rests, and from which it concludes to the existence of an *Ens a se,* immutable by His very nature. . . .

Science, philosophy and Revelation

The knowledge of God as sole Creator, now shared by many modern scientists, is indeed the extreme limit to which human reason can attain. Nevertheless, as you are well aware, it does not constitute the last frontier of Truth. In harmonious cooperation, because all three are instruments of truth, like rays of the same sun, science, philosophy and, with still greater reason, Revelation, contemplate the substance of this Creator whom science has met along its path, unveil His outlines and point out His features. . . .

Distinct from the world, but not outside

This Divine Spirit is distinct and different from the world but not outside of the world, nor secluded as it were in disdainful isolation and abandoning His own handiworks to themselves, as the deistic theories would have it.

Rather, this Divine Spirit is present in the world which He omnipotently creates, conserves and governs; to Him an essential dependence binds the world in its intimate being and operation.

The breath of goodness and love

. . . to the mind of the scientist who knows how to find a meaning in the totality of existing reality, this Divine Spirit reveals Himself not as the cold cosmos, but as the breath of goodness and love which pervades all and explains all, and which in a particular way concentrates itself and reveals itself in the human creature made to His own image and likeness. Hence it is that this Divine

Spirit does not disdain to make man the constant object of His ineffable loving operation, such as the Redemption by means of the mystery of His Incarnation.

Modern concepts and the Incarnation

The subsequent development of man's concepts of the universe—which has rightly overturned the ancient geocentric and anthropocentric ideas, has contracted our planet to the dimensions of microscopic star-dust, and has shrunk man to the size of an atom on this bit of dust, confining both in a corner of the universe—does not constitute an obstacle, as some have claimed, in discussing the mystery of the Incarnation, either for the love or the omnipotence of Him Who is pure spirit and as such possesses an infinite superiority to matter, whatever be its cosmic dimensions in space, time, mass and energy.

An Apostolic Benediction

. . . besides the profound esteem which We cherish for your [scientists of World Astronomical Congress] science and for all other sciences, a further motive, looking toward higher and universal horizons, incites Us to formulate these good wishes for you.

May the modern conception of astronomical science, which has been the goal of so many scholars of the past, like Copernicus, Galileo, Kepler and Newton, remain still fruitful of further marvelous progress in modern astrophysics; and, thanks to the peaceful collaboration of which the International Astronomical Union is a shining example, may the astronomical picture of the universe become ever more and more perfect.

And in order that the eternal light of God may guide and illuminate your studies, which are directed toward revealing the traces of His perfection and toward hearing the echoes of His harmonies, We invoke on all here present the celestial favors, in pledge of which may there descend upon you Our Apostolic Benediction.

Genetics and eugenics

The fundamental tendency of genetics and eugenics is to influence the transmission of hereditary factors so as to promote what is good and eliminate what is harmful. This basic tendency is irreproachable from a moral point of view. . . .

To the number of measures which are harmful to morality, including "racism," . . . must be added eugenic sterilization. . . .

Other paths lead to the same goal: the prohibition of marriage or its physical impossibility through segregation for those whose heredity is defective must be equally rejected. The objective sought is good in itself, but the means of obtaining it impair the personal right to contract and consummate marriage.

When the bearer of a heredity taint is not capable of conducting himself humanly, and is, consequently, incapable of contracting marriage, or if later should become incapable of claiming by means of a free act the right acquired through valid marriage, then he can be lawfully prevented from procreating a new life. Outside of these cases the prohibition of marriage and matrimonial relations for biological, genetic or eugenic reasons is unjust, whoever imposes such a prohibition, whether it be a private person or a public authority.

Certainly a person has a right and, in most cases, a duty to point out to those who are unquestionably bearers of a markedly defective heredity what a burden they are about to impose on themselves, their spouses and their offspring. It is a burden that may become intolerable. But to advise against is not to forbid. There may be other motives, particularly of a moral or personal nature, which are so preponderant as to authorize the contraction and consummation of marriage, even under the circumstances already indicated.

Noble and worthy aims

The practical aims of genetics are noble and worthy of being recognized and encouraged. May it always remain conscious in the evaluation of the means used to realize those ends of the fundamental difference between the vegetable and animal world on the one hand and man on the other. In the first, the means for the improvement of species and races are at its complete disposal. In the second, in the world of man, it has always before it personal beings who have intangible rights, individuals who on their side are governed by inflexible moral laws when they exercise their faculty of creating new life. Thus, the Creator Himself has established certain barriers in the moral sphere which no human power may break down.

Philosophy cannot ignore genetics

Genetics, as such, can have nothing to say on the fact that a spiritual soul is joined in the unity of human nature to an organic substratum which enjoys a relative autonomy. Psychology and metaphysics or ontology ought to intervene here, not to oppose genetics but together with it to substantially further and complete its findings. On the other hand, philosophy can no longer ignore genetics if, in the analysis of psychic activity, it wants to remain in contact with reality. One cannot hope to deduce all psychic activity, since it is conditioned by the body, from the "anima rationalis" as "forma corporis" and assert that the amorphous "material prima" is entirely determined by the spiritual soul, created immediately by God, and receiving nothing from the genes contained in the cellular nucleus.

The sciences of man

But in our days, without ceasing to study nature, we are turning more and more toward the sciences of man and particularly toward those whose object is human society. Here, given the intervention of personal and free causes, a great number of facts escape appraisal by classical mathematical analysis and seem to defy all attempts at rational and systematic explanation. . . .

Contribution of the science of statistics

If you [statisticians] are making a great contribution to the study of present-day society, whose rapid evolution calls for constant work at putting it into focus and forecasting its trends, the great international problems are also profiting from the application of your methods. In particular, one sees today whole populations suddenly given access to culture and insistently demanding major improvements in their material and intellectual standard of living. The institutions whose task it is to help them need information that will enable them to consider exact data on the question. Here again statistics intervene to direct such efforts and here also are you carrying on a work the importance of which We are pleased to emphasize.

Statistics and truth

There is one point on which We wish to insist again since, it might be said, it conditions all the rest of your work [statistics]. Since statistics proposes to give the most exact information possible, within the limits of its own methods, we expect from the person who practices it, besides the professional competence We mentioned above, a loyalty and sincerity which is above all suspicion. It is useless to perfect methods if in the end they will serve only to deceive the public more efficiently. Now the temptation is great, when there is a strong desire to support a thesis, to twist results in a certain way, to dissimulate the truth or even, for financial gain or propaganda purposes, to falsify embarrassing or damaging results. Be on your guard and do not give in to this temptation and thus degrade your profession. To the love of truth, which is the very soul of scientific work, unite rectitude of conscience, which rejects all compromise and which—to repeat it once more—carefully distinguishes between statistical data and the results deduced from them.

Regarding the doctrine of evolution

. . . the teaching authority of the Church does not forbid that in conformity with the present state of human sciences and sacred theology, research and discussions on the part of men experienced in both fields take place with regard to the doctrine of evolution in as far as it inquires into the origin of the human body as coming from pre-existent and living matter—for Catholic Faith obliges us to hold that souls are immediately created by God. . . .

Nothing dearer. . . .

I follow with intense interest your [members of the École Française] research in history and archeology which you achieve in archives and in your excavations, because you work to discover the truth and the light. And could there be anything dearer to Our heart and to the Church than the light and the truth? For the Church has nothing to gain by spreading false legends, nothing to lose by revealing what really has happened.

Scientists and a new world order

We are fully confident that the present generation of natural scientists may still be able to employ all their intellectual powers and all their idealism to found a new world order of justice and of peace, with the collaboration of all decent men of all countries; an order which excludes everything extreme, evil and unjust; an order which the Italian people, too, with their deep faith, will be able to welcome with joy. The day on which scientists can take up this gigantic task of reconstruction in the service of mankind will be a day of pure and lasting joy. . . .

[XI]

Technology

"IT IS UNDENIABLE," says Pius XII, "that technological progress comes from God, and so it can and ought to lead to God." Far from turning one's back on the marvels of technology and its lawful use, if one is a believer he "may find himself more eager to bow his knee." The believer will even find it natural to place the conquests of technology alongside the gold, frankincense and myrrh offered by the Magi to the infant God. The welcoming attitude of the Pope in regard to technology is beautifully expressed when he says that "men can at last say that they have in some measure fulfilled the divine command!"—the command uttered in Genesis, "Inhabit the earth and subdue it."

But the Pope severely castigates the "technological concept" of life, which sets up technology as a new idol to be worshipped, and from which many seek salvation. The "technological spirit" is a spirit which relies on the technicians' production and organization to solve all problems, even confounding the boundless panorama unfolded by technology with the infinite itself. It has blurred man's perception of the "profound realities of organic life, and even more so those of the spiritual life, the living realities of the individual person and of human society." And it also arrests in man intellectual life itself, while making him insensible to the Divine.

R. C. P.

Domination of the natural world

Technology has in fact brought man's domination of the natural world to a pitch of perfection never known before. The modern machine allows a mode of production that substitutes for, and multiplies a hundredfold, human energy for work, that is entirely independent of the contribution of organic forces and which ensures a maximum of extensive and intensive potential and at the same time of precision. As We embrace with a glance the results of this development, nature itself seems to give an assent of satisfaction to what has been done in it, and to incite to further investigation and use of its extraordinary possibilities. Now it is clear that all search for and discovery of the forces of nature, which technology effectuates, is at once a search for and discovery of the greatness, of the wisdom and of the harmony of God. Looked at in this way, there is nothing to disapprove of or condemn in technology.

A gift from God

From Our words, directed against the materialism of the past century and of the present time, it would be wrong to deduce a condemnation of technical progress.

No, We do not condemn that which is a gift of God, Who, just as He causes the bread-yielding wheat to rise from the sod of the earth, has also hidden in the bowels of the earth from the

(126)

time of the world's creation treasures of fire, of metals, of precious stones to be uncovered by the hand of man for his needs, for his works and for his progress.

Technology its own avenger

The Church, mother of so many universities of Europe, while continuing to exalt and gather together the most fearless masters of the sciences and explorers of nature, does not fail at the same time to bear in mind that all God's gifts and the very freedom of the human will itself can be used in a way to merit praise and reward, or blame and condemnation. Thus, it has happened that the spirit and the tendency with which technical progress was often put to use have brought it about that in our time technology must expiate its error and be, as it were, its own avenger by producing instruments of destruction which destroy today what it has erected yesterday.

Hateful abuses

. . . We need not seek far, or go back far, to find concrete examples of these hateful abuses [of knowledge and God's gifts in nature]. For example, the disintegration of the atom and the production of atomic energy is one thing; but it is a different thing to use it for destruction beyond all control. The magnificent progress of the most modern techniques in aviation is one thing; but the wide employment of squadrons of bombers, without the possibility of limiting their action to military and strategic objectives, is quite another. It is one thing to engage in respectful investigation revealing the beauty of God in the mirror of His works, and His power in the force of nature; but it is quite another thing to deify that nature and its material forces through the denial of their Author.

Technology can bring blessings

. . . A gift of God by its very nature, today's ultrapowerful technology becomes, in the hands of violent men of parties ruling with the brutality of force, of omnipotent and oppressor states, a terrible instrument of injustice, slavery and cruelty. And in modern warfare it intensifies to an intolerable degree the sufferings and torments of the populations. On the other hand, restrained and directed by a society which fears God, which obeys His precepts and esteems spiritual, moral and eternal things incomparably more than the material, technology can bring us those blessings for which it was ordained according to the Creator's design.

Gold, frankincense and myrrh

Very far then from any thought of disavowing the marvels of technology and its lawful use, the believer may find himself more eager to bow his knee. . . He will even find it natural to place beside the gold, frankincense and myrrh, offered by the Magi to the infant God, also the modern conquests of technology; machines and numbers, laboratories and inventions, power and resources. Furthermore, such an offering is like presenting Him with the work which He Himself once commanded and which is now being effected, though it has not yet reached its term. "Inhabit the earth and subdue it" (Gen. i, 28), said God to man as He handed creation over to him in temporary heritage. What a long and hard road from then to the present day, when men can at last say that they have in some measure fulfilled the divine command!

The people welcome technological progress

. . . The people have welcomed, and rightly so, technological progress, because it eases the burden of toil and increases production. But it also must be admitted that if such a way of thinking is not kept within right bounds, the human and Christian concept of work necessarily becomes distorted. Likewise, from this distorted concept of life and hence of work, men come to consider leisure time as an end in itself, instead of looking upon it and using it as reasonable rest and recreation, bound up essentially with the rhythm of an ordered life, in which rest and toil alternate in a single pattern and are integrated into a single harmony.

The rudder has slipped

One would say that humanity today, which has been able to build the marvelous, complex machine of the modern world, subjugating to its service the tremendous forces of nature, now appears incapable of controlling these forces—as though the rudder has slipped from its hands—and so it is in peril of being overthrown and crushed by them.

Such inability to control should of itself suggest to men who are its victims not to expect salvation solely from the technicians' production and organization. The work of these can help, and notably, to solve the grave and extensive problems which afflict the world only if it is bound up with, and directed toward, bettering and strengthening true human values, but in no case—oh, how We wish that all, both on this continent and beyond the sea, would realize it—will it avail to fashion a world without misery.

A tormented age

. . . What age has been, for all its technical and purely civic progress, more tormented than ours by spiritual emptiness and deep-felt
interior poverty? May we not, perhaps, apply to it the prophetic
words of the Apocalypse: "Thou sayest: I am rich, and made
wealthy, and have need of nothing: and knowest not, that thou
art wretched, and miserable, and poor, and blind, and naked?"
(Apoc. iii, 17)

The technical concept of society

One knows where to look in social thought for the technical
concept of society: in the gigantic enterprises of modern industry.
We do not intend here to express an opinion on the necessity,
utility and disadvantages of these forms of production. Indubitably
they are marvelous manifestations of the inventive and constructive
genius of the human spirit. It is right for the world to admire enterprises which in the area of production and management succeed
in coordinating and mobilizing the physical forces of men and
matter. And the present age may take legitimate pride in the stable
way in which these enterprises are organized and in the often
novel and characteristic beauty of their external set-up. But what
must be denied is that modern social life should be regulated by
them or made to conform to them.

The "technological spirit"

. . . it can hardly be denied that this technology, which in our
century has reached the height of its splendor and fruitfulness,
is, through certain circumstances, changed to a grave spiritual

danger. For it seems to give modern man, prostrate at its altar, a sense of self-sufficiency and satisfaction to his boundless thirst for knowledge and power. In its many varied uses, in the absolute confidence which it awakens, in the extraordinary possibilities that it promises, modern technology displays before man so vast a vision as to be confounded by many with the infinite itself. In consequence, it is allowed an inadmissible autonomy, which in turn is translated in the thoughts of some into a false conception of life and of the world, known as the "technological spirit."

In what exactly does this spirit consist? In this, that what is most highly prized in human life is the advantage that can be drawn from the forces and elements of nature; whatever is technically possible in mechanical production takes precedence over all other forms of human activity, and the perfection of earthly culture and happiness is seen in it.

The "technological concept of life"

The "technological concept of life" is therefore nothing else than a particular form of materialism, in as far as it offers a mathematical formula and utilitarian calculations as the ultimate answer to the question of existence. . . .

A distorted vision

There is a fundamental falsehood in this distorted vision of the world offered by the technological spirit. The seemingly boundless panorama unfolded before the eyes of modern man, however extensive it may be, remains but a partial projection of life on reality, only expressing its relations with matter. Accordingly, it is a deceitful panorama, that finishes by shutting up as in a prison those who are too credulous with regard to the omnipotence and immensity of technology; a prison which is vast, indeed, but nevertheless circumscribed, and hence in the long run insupportable to their true spirit. Their glance, far from reaching out over infinite reality as they thought (for reality does not consist only of matter), will feel chafed by the barriers which matter of necessity imposes. From this results the deep anguish of contemporary man, made blind for having wilfully surrounded himself with darkness.

"Progress in technology"

It is to these men whose spirit is in darkness that We wish to point out "the great light" radiating from the manger, asking them above all else to realize the cause which in our time is making them blind and insensible to the Divine. It is the excessive, and sometimes exclusive, esteem for what is called "progress in technology." This dream was first cherished as the omnipotent myth and dispenser of happiness; then pushed forward by every device to the most daring conquests; and it has finally imposed itself on the minds of men as the final end of man and of life, substituting itself, therefore, for every kind of religious and spiritual ideal. But now it is becoming ever clearer that its undue exploitation has so blinded men's intelligence that they exemplify in themselves what the *Book of Wisdom* castigated in the men of its time (Wisdom xiii, 1): they are incapable of learning from the visible world of Him Who is, of discovering the worker from His work. . . .

Nevertheless, the aforementioned erroneous consequence does not follow necessarily, nor are Our present criticisms to be understood as a condemnation of technological progress in itself. The Church loves and favors human progress. It is undeniable that technological progress comes from God, and so it can and ought to lead to God. In point of fact, while the believer admires the conquests of science and makes use of them to penetrate more deeply into the knowledge of creation and of the forces of nature, that by means of machines he may better master them for the service of mankind and the enrichment of human life, it most often happens that he feels himself drawn to adore the Giver of those good things which he admires and uses. . . .

The profound realities of organic life

It is evident that whoever adopts the method of technology as the sole way of seeking truth must give up any ideal of penetrating the profound realities of organic life, and even more so those of the spiritual life, the living realities of the individual person and of human society, because these cannot be analyzed into quantitative relationships. . . .

Restricting the free expansion of the intelligence

. . . Even leaving aside the religious blindness which comes from this "technological spirit," a man who is possessed by it is arrested in his intellectual life, and yet it is precisely in that life that man is created to the image of God. God's intellect is infinitely comprehensive, whereas the "technological spirit" makes every effort to restrict in man the free expansion of his intelligence.

"Admirable is the Divine Wisdom"

"Every good gift and every perfect gift is from above, coming down from the Father of Lights. . . ." (James i, 17). To the Wisdom of God, then, our tribute of admiration is due for those many inventions of modern science which make it possible for men to use electric energy to communicate with one another from a distance. Admirable is the Divine Wisdom which empowers them to telegraph their messages to the absent at a moment's notice; to converse by long-distance telephone; to broadcast their information over the ether waves; to picture, lastly, on the television screen before their eyes what actually is happening far away.

Radio, image of the Apostolic Faith

. . . the Marconi Radio—whose voice is heard in an instant round the world—marvelous invention and eloquent image of the Apostolic Faith that embraces all mankind. . . .

Spanning the world

. . . We greet . . . this most expedite bridge [the radio] which the inventive genius of our age throws across the ether in a flash, to unite across mountains, seas, and continents every corner of the earth. . . .

Thanks to modern technology. . . .

Thanks to modern technology We are able to speak directly to many who are ill and We hope that we shall be able to reach in other ways those who cannot hear Our voice. Certainly we wish We had the omnipresence of God. . . .

Instrument of truth

. . . We are convinced of the vital importance of so effective a means of communication [as the radio] in the battle that the Church is waging with peaceful arms under all the heavens in behalf of authentic truth, indispensable morality, strict justice, and sincere love not only between men, but between nations as well.

The good results are incalculable

One sometimes hears complaints about the sins of radio and how it perverts minds and manners. Because the gifts of God and the discoveries of men are sometimes abused, must one deprive oneself and others of their benefits ordained by Providence? One must indeed condemn and denounce abuses; one must seek the most efficacious measures to repress them. But one must appreciate the advances each generation makes and see to it that their good results, thanks to wise and conscientious men, surpass and neutralize the evil wrought by unworthy exploiters.

These good results are incalculable and touch every field. Even from a purely practical viewpoint, who could sing sufficiently the praises of the immense service rendered by broadcasting in a case of urgent distress or extreme danger? Who could describe sufficiently the social usefulness of the information given in the communications exchanged between all the members of the great human family? Who could estimate the profit to general culture brought about by the possibility of letting people hear talks and instructions on the most varied subjects, of allowing people to taste the elevating charms of good diction and beautiful music?

St. Gabriel Archangel, Patron of Telecommunications

Technical instruments of this kind, it is true, can do a great deal of harm if they are not put to use with honest intent. But just as clearly they can render precious service in many ways when properly employed. They may promote the brotherhood of man and human culture. They may contribute to the spread of the liberal arts, and of scientific research throughout the world. They may even serve to impart religious instruction, to carry the voice of the Supreme Pastor of souls from St. Peter's to the farthest corners of the earth, and to unite in wondrous manner the hearts and minds and voices of the faithful everywhere in public prayer to the Divine Majesty.

That will explain why Holy Mother Church has never for an instant opposed the development of this widespread practice. Nay, she has been at pains to foster, stimulate and protect it in the fullest measure possible, and still continues to do so. She has, indeed, good reason to know that every truth, every new scientific discovery must be welcomed as one more trace, as it were, of the Divine Intelligence, and one more token of the power of God.

We believe it to be most opportune, therefore, that these marvelous professions, with their technical staffs and assistants, should enjoy the advantage of a heavenly blessing and a supernatural protection all their own. . . .

We do now, by virtue of these Letters, appoint and proclaim St. Gabriel Archangel to be henceforth and forever the Heavenly Patron before God of the above professions and their members, with all of the liturgical honors and privileges to which principal Patrons of their type are entitled. . . .

For good and evil

The rapid progress which television has already made in many countries draws Our attention more and more to this marvelous instrument which science and technology offer humanity, destined as it is to have a profound influence for good or evil on public and private life.

No one has the right. . . .

. . . No one has the right to watch passively the rapid developments in television, when he realizes the extremely powerful influence it undoubtedly can exercise on the national life, either in promoting good or in spreading evil.

Possibilities of television

Neither may We be indifferent to the beneficial consequences which television can have in social matters, in relation to culture, to popular education, to teaching in the school and in the international life of peoples, for it will certainly help them to a greater mutual knowledge and understanding and promote more cordial feelings and better reciprocal cooperation.

Thanks to God

. . . television, too, obliges Us all to gratitude, a duty which the Church never wearies of inculcating in her children every day in the Holy Sacrifice of the Mass, telling them that "it is really worthy and just, right and salutary, always and everywhere to give thanks to God" for His gifts.

Television and the family

In recent times the cinema, sports, not to mention the dire necessities of daily work, have increasingly tended to keep members of the family away from home, and thus the natural blossoming of domestic life has been upset. We must be glad, then, that television contributes efficaciously to re-establish the balance, by providing the whole family with an opportunity for honest diversion together. . . .

The world in the home

Different from the theater and the cinema, which limit their plays to those who attend of their own free choice, television is directed especially to family groups, made up of persons of every age, of both sexes, of differing education and moral training. Into that circle it brings the newspaper, the chronicle of events, the drama. Like the radio it can enter at any time, any home and any place, bringing not only sounds and words but the detailed vividness and action of pictures; which makes it more capable of moving the emotions, especially of youth. . . .

It is easy, therefore, to realize how television is very intimately bound up with the education of youth and even the sanctity of the home.

[XII]

Medicine

IN DEALING WITH the pressing problems raised by medical research and treatment, the Holy Father does so in his usual positive manner, for he has a profound appreciation of the advances underlying these problems, and their spiritual possibilities. And here again he shows us that a truly spiritual approach has a transfiguring effect, in filling us with delight before values which the progress of science has brought into the limelight. Thus, guided by the Pope, we discover that so far from frustrating the admiration for human achievement which so spontaneously arises within us, a genuinely spiritual attitude gives it greater amplitude.

The new knowledge gained by medical science is good in itself. For as Pius XII has said, "the free expansion of the intelligence" is natural to man who has been made to the image of a God whose "intellect is infinitely comprehensive." If knowledge in itself were not a positive value, "omniscience would not be a divine attribute." But science, after all, is not the only value, for it belongs within an order of values, and in this order it is not supreme. Hence there are well-defined limits which even medical science cannot transgress without violating higher moral rules. The moral demands do not act as an obstacle to science, for they force the impetuous stream of human thought and will "to flow, like water from the mountains into certain channels. They contain the flow to increase its efficiency and usefulness."

R. C. P.

A noble and sublime vocation

. . . His [the doctor's] vocation is noble, sublime; his responsibility to society is grave; but God will not fail to bless him for his charity and for his unstinting, devoted efforts to alleviate the sufferings of his fellow-man on earth. . . .

The progress of medicine

For many centuries, and especially during our own age, the progress of medicine is obvious. It is a progress certainly complex and embracing the most varied branches of theory and practice: progress in the study of the body and the organism, in all the physical, chemical and natural sciences; in the knowledge of medicines, their properties and their use; progress in applying to the art of healing not only the science of physiology but also of psychology; of the mutual actions and reactions of physics, and of morality.

The doctor who is worthy of his vocation

What . . . does the medical doctor worthy of his vocation do? He dominates these same forces, these natural properties, in order to obtain from them healing, health and vigor, and often, what is even more precious, prevention of illness and preservation from infection and epidemic. In his hands the formidable power of radioactivity is harnessed and controlled for the cure of diseases resisting all other treatment. The properties of poisons, even the most virulent, serve for the preparation of the most efficacious medicines. Even the germs of infection are employed in all manner of ways in serotherapy and in vaccination.

Zeal for humanity

If the simple zeal for humanity, the natural love for one's fellow-men, spurs and guides every conscientious medical doctor in all his research, what is there that the Christian doctor will not do when, moved by Divine charity, he dedicates himself, without sparing either his efforts or himself, for the good of those whom he rightly regards in faith as his brethren? He certainly rejoices wholeheartedly in the immense progress already made, and the results already obtained by his predecessors and continued today by his colleagues, with whom he joins to continue a magnificent tradition. He is justly proud of making his own contribution.

The Catholic doctor

Never . . . does he [the Catholic doctor] consider himself satisfied; he is always looking to the future, to new distances to cover, to new advances to be made. He works enthusiastically both as a medical doctor, wholly dedicated to obtain alleviation for humanity and each individual, and as a scientist whom consequent discoveries give a taste of the joy of learning. He is a believer and a Christian who, in the splendors he discovers in the new horizons that open before him, sees the greatness and power of the Creator, the inexhaustible goodness of the Father, who, after having given the living organism so many resources for its development, its defense and in most cases for its spontaneous healing, leads him again to find in nature, inert or living, mineral, vegetable or animal, the remedies for bodily ills.

The ideal of his vocation

The medical doctor would not be corresponding fully to the ideal of his vocation if—while profiting from the most recent advances of the medical science and art—he used as a practitioner merely his intelligence and his ability, and if he did not also make use (and We were about to say, above all) of his heart as a man, and of his loving tenderness as a Christian.

Precious creature

. . . the doctor is not handling inert matter, however priceless. Suffering in his hands is a human creature, a man like himself. Like himself that patient has a post of duty in some family where loving hearts are anxiously awaiting him; he has a mission to fulfill, even though humble, in human society. What is more, that ailing, crippled, paling form has a rendezvous with eternity. . . . Precious creature of God's love and omnipotence!

Spirit and dust: image of the infinite

Spirit and dust compounded to form an image of the Infinite; living in time and space, yet headed toward a goal that lies beyond both; part of the created universe, yet destined to share the glory and joy of the Creator, that man who places himself in the care of a doctor is something more than nerves and tissue, blood and organs. . . .

Value of scientific knowledge

Scientific knowledge has its own value in the domain of medical science no less than in other scientific domains, such as, for example, physics, chemistry, cosmology and psychology. It is a value which must certainly not be minimized, a value existing quite independently of the usefulness or use of the acquired knowledge. Moreover, knowledge as such and the full understanding of any truth raise no moral objection. By virtue of this principle, research and the acquisition of truth for arriving at new, wider and deeper knowledge and understanding of the same truth are in themselves in accord with the moral order.

Knowledge, a positive value

. . . knowledge in itself is always a positive value, in medicine as well as in all other branches. If it were not, omniscience could not be a divine attribute. . . . But if the growth of knowledge is good in itself, it does not follow that all means of acquiring it are legitimate. In a general way, moreover, not all knowledge is suitable for all men or even all groups of men. Knowledge is certainly not good when one perversely intends to use it to harm others or to wrong them unjustly.

Science is not the supreme value

But this [the fact that scientific knowledge has its own value] does not mean that all methods, or any single method, arrived at by scientific and technical research offers every moral guarantee. Nor, moreover, does it mean that every method becomes licit because it increases and deepens our knowledge. Sometimes it happens that a method cannot be used without injuring the rights of others or without violating some moral rule of absolute value. In such a case, although one rightly envisages and pursues the increase of knowledge, morally the method is not admissible. Why not? Because science is not the highest value, that to which all other orders of values—or in the same order of value, all particular values—should be subordinated. . . .

Science is within an order of values

. . . Science itself, therefore, as well as its research and acquisitions, must be inserted in the order of values. Here there are well defined limits which even medical science cannot transgress without violating higher moral rules. The confidential relations between doctor and patient, the personal right of the patient to the life of his body and soul in its psychic and moral integrity are just some of the many values superior to scientific interest. . . .

Two precious objects

. . . Conscious as you [Surgeons] are of your responsibility, you realize that it derives from the fact, dominant in this matter from beginning to end, that in the exercise of your profession it is human persons whom you hold in your hands and under your knives. They are persons whose living body merits all your respect as it has a right to your every professional care. Even when life itself is not at stake, you have at your disposition—as you are fully aware—two precious objects: the integrity of the human body and the mysterious reality of human suffering.

. . . God alone is Lord of the life and integrity of man, Lord as to members, his organs, his potencies, and particularly of those which make him an associate in the work of creation. . . .

Man is not the absolute owner of his body

. . . man is not really the absolute owner and master of his body, but only has the use of it; and God cannot permit him to use it in a manner contrary to the intrinsic and natural purpose which He has assigned as the function of the diverse parts.

The bold spirit of research

. . . The bold spirit of research incites one to follow newly discovered roads, to extend them, to create new ones and to renew methods. A serious, competent doctor will often see with a sort of spontaneous intuition the moral legality of what he proposes to do and will act according to his conscience. But there are other instances where he does not have this security, where he may see or think he sees the contrary with certainty or where he doubts and wavers between Yes and No. In the most serious and profound matters, the man in the physician is not content with examining from a medical point of view what he can attempt and succeed in. He also wants to see his way clearly in regard to moral possibilities and obligations.

Natural and Christian morality. . . .

Natural and Christian morality maintains . . . everywhere its imprescriptible rights and it is from these, and not from any consideration of feelings or of materialistic and naturalistic philanthropy that the essential principles of medical deontology (the science of duty or moral obligation) are derived: such as the dignity of the human body, the pre-eminence of the soul over the body, the brotherhood of all men, the sovereign domain of God over life and destiny.

Exact scientific knowledge and morality

. . . without exact knowledge of the medical facts it is impossible to determine what moral principle applies to the treatment under discussion. The doctor, therefore, looks at the medical aspect of the case, the moralist, the laws of morality. Ordinarily, when explained and completed mutually, the medical and moral evidence will make possible a reliable decision as to the moral legality of the case in all its concrete aspects.

Three guiding principles

In order to justify the morality of new procedures, new attempts and methods of research and medical treatment, three main principles must be kept in mind: 1. the interests of medical science; 2. the interests of the individual patient to be treated; 3. the interests of the community, the "bonum commune" (common good).

Dangers and risks

Without doubt, before giving moral authorization to the use of new methods, one cannot ask that any danger or any risk be excluded. That would exceed human possibilities, paralyze all serious scientific research and very frequently be to the detriment of the patient. In these cases the weighing of the danger must be left to the judgment of the tried and competent doctor. Nevertheless, as Our explanation has shown, there is a degree of danger that morality cannot allow. In doubtful cases, when means already known have failed, it may happen that a new method still insufficiently tried offers, together with very dangerous elements, appreciable chances of success. If the patient gives his consent, the use of the procedure in question is licit. But this way of acting cannot be upheld as a line of conduct in normal cases.

Moral demands do not constitute a brake

People will perhaps object that the ideas set forth here present a serious obstacle to scientific research and work. Nevertheless, the limits We have outlined are not by definition an obstacle to progress. The field of medicine cannot be different in this respect from other fields of man's research, investigations and work. The great moral demands force the impetuous flow of human thought and will to flow, like water from the mountains, into certain channels. They contain the flow to increase its efficiency and usefulness. They dam it so that it does not overflow and cause ravages that can never be compensated for by the special good it seeks. In appearance, moral demands are a brake. In fact, they contribute to the best and most beautiful of what man has produced for science, the individual and the community.

May Almighty God in His benevolent Providence give you His blessing and grace to this end.

[XIII]

Psychotherapy

"THE CHURCH," declares Pius XII, "looks with satisfaction at the new paths opened by psychiatry in this postwar period." For, as he also says, it is "capable of achieving precious results for medicine, for the knowledge of the soul in general, for the religious dispositions of man and for their development." The Pope also tells us that the mobilization of science for the conquest of mental illness is welcomed by the Church, because She knows that the recovery of a spirit from mental illness is "like the first step toward gaining him for Christ. For it affords him the possibility of becoming for the first time a conscious and active member of His Mystical Body, or of returning to such active membership from an atrophied, inert condition."

However, the intense concentration on the psychic dynamisms by depth psychology makes it necessary to hold aloft an easily forgotten truth, namely, that "existential" man in his inmost structure is identified with "essential" man. That is, man in the concrete with his psychic dynamisms cannot be separated from man as we know him, in his full constitution as a being endowed with intellect and will and manifesting a tendency to the infinite. Hence the folly of dealing with man as though his sexual life were identical with the whole of human life itself. Hence, too, the absurdity of overlooking a real sense of guilt because we often find an unhealthy sense of guilt. For, in the full constitution of man's life, the perception of truth and value is paramountly real, and so is conscience.

R. C. P.

Recent psychological discoveries

Science affirms that recent observations have brought to light the hidden layers of the psychic structure of man, and it tries to understand the meaning of these discoveries, to interpret them and render them capable of use. People speak of dynamisms, determinisms and mechanisms hidden in the depth of the soul, endowed with immanent laws whence are derived certain modes of acting. Undoubtedly these begin to operate within the subconscious or the unconscious, but they also penetrate into the realms of the conscious and determine it. People claim to have devised methods that have been tried and recognized as adequate to scrutinize the mystery of the depths of the soul, to elucidate them and put them back on the right road when they are exercising a harmful influence.

These questions, which lend themselves to the examination of scientific psychology, belong to your competence. The same may be said for the use of new psychic methods. But theoretical and practical psychology, the one as much as the other, should bear in mind that they cannot lose sight of the truths established by reason and by faith, nor of the obligatory precepts of ethics.

Conquest of mental illness

In the face of this wide mobilization of science and public authority for the conquest of the social malady of mental illness, We, moved not only by the profound human sympathy which such sufferers inspire, but also by religious considerations, desire to express Our particular pleasure at all that has been done and is now being planned by societies, organizations, leagues—some of them world-wide. . . .

The Church looks with satisfaction. . . .

. . . If mental health enjoys such esteem in Catholic thought and practice, it is only right that the Church looks with satisfaction at the new paths being opened by psychiatry in this postwar period. It knows that the recovery of a spirit from insanity, whether by prevention or by cure, is like the first step toward gaining him for Christ. For it affords him the possibility of becoming for the first time a conscious and active member of His Mystical Body, or of returning to such active membership from an atrophied, inert condition.

The priest and the doctor

. . . Nowadays, in certain pathological cases, it is not rare for the priest to send his penitent to a doctor. . . .

A healthy mind and religious development

That mental health is one of the fundamental goods from the viewpoint of nature is obvious. But, it is just as clear that such health is also fundamental in the religious and supernatural sphere.

In fact, the full development of religious values and of Christian sanctity in a soul is inconceivable, if a man does not start out with a healthy mind, well-balanced in its activities. On the other hand, it is equally certain that no physical defect or impairment can hinder the achievement of the most exalted sanctity. Is it really necessary to recall the great esteem in which mental health is held in Christian thought and practice? All that Sacred Scripture says in praise of Wisdom and of mere human wisdom—which is to be preferred to physical strength, to kingdoms, to riches (cf. Wisdom vi, 1 and pass.)—is an implicit affirmation of the importance of psychical presuppositions, or rather of mental health. . . .

Man's charter

Man is an ordered unit and whole, a microcosm, a sort of state whose charter, determined by the end of the whole, subordinates to this end the activity of the parts according to the true order of their value and function. This charter is, in the final analysis, of an ontological and metaphysical origin, not a psychological and personal one. There are those who have thought it necessary to accentuate the opposition between the metaphysical and the psychological. A completely wrong approach! The psychic itself belongs to the domain of the ontological and metaphysical.

Basic points

The fundamental orientation of a Christian psychologist and psychiatrist toward man must be such as to consider him: (1) as a psychical unity and totality; (2) as a unity with a complete structure of its own; (3) as a social unity; and (4) as a transcendental unity, or in his tendency toward God.

It is clear that this last consideration, not infrequently passed over because of the survival of naturalistic currents, ought to be held in high regard. . . .

Tendency to the infinite

It pertains to the technique of your science [psychotherapy] to clarify the questions of the existence, the structure and the mode of action of this dynamism [a dynamism which, rooted in the depths of the psychic being, would push man toward the infinite . . . an effective impulse carrying man to the Divine]. If its outcome proves to be positive, it should not be declared irreconcilable with reason or faith. This would only show that, even in its deepest roots, *esse ab alio* [to be from another], also implies *esse ad alium* [to be for another], and that St. Augustine's words: "Thou hast made us for Thyself, O Lord, and our heart shall not rest until it rests in Thee" (Confessions, Book I, chapter 1, N.1), find a new confirmation in the very depths of man's psychic being. Even if there were question of a dynamism involving all men, peoples, epochs and cultures, what a help and what an invaluable help this would be for the search after God and the affirmation of His existence!

Misunderstandings

. . . We should certainly not find fault with depth psychology if it deals with the psychic aspect of religious phenomena and endeavors to analyze and reduce it to a scientific system, even if this research is new and if its terminology is not found in the past. We mention this point, because misunderstandings can easily arise when psychology attributes new meanings to already accepted expressions. Prudence and reserve are needed on both sides in order to avoid false interpretations and to make it possible to reach a reciprocal understanding.

Primacy of the whole man

. . . The various psychic faculties and functions form part of the whole spiritual being and subordinate themselves to its final end. . . .

Psychic dynamisms and the soul

. . . the existence of each psychic faculty and function is explained by the end of the whole man. What constitutes man is principally the soul, the substantial form of his nature. From it, ultimately, flows all the vital activity of man. In it are rooted all the psychic dynamisms with their own proper structure and their organic law. It is the soul which nature charges with the government of all man's energies, in so far as these have not yet acquired their final determination.

Given this ontological and psychological fact, it follows that it would be a departure from reality to attempt, in theory or in practice, to entrust the determining role of the whole to one particular factor, for example, to one of the elementary psychic dynamisms, and thus install a secondary power at the helm. These psychic dynamisms may be *in* the soul, *in* man. They are not, however, the soul nor the man. They are energies of considerable intensity perhaps, but nature has entrusted their direction to the center-post, to the spiritual soul endowed with intellect and will, which is normally capable of governing these energies. That these energies may exercise pressure upon one activity does not necessarily signify that they compel it. To deprive the soul of its central place would be to deny an ontological and psychic reality.

Real guilt and a morbid sense of guilt

. . . No one will deny that there can exist—and not infrequently—an irrational and even morbid sense of guilt. But a person may also be aware of a real fault which has not been wiped away.

The pansexual method

It is not proved—it is, in fact, incorrect—that the pansexual method of a certain school of psychoanalysis is an indispensable integrating part of all psychotherapy which is serious and worthy of the name. . . .

A moral limit

. . . In order to rid himself of repressions, inhibitions or psychic complexes, man is not free to arouse in himself for therapeutic purposes each and every appetite of a sexual order which is being excited or has been excited in his being, appetites whose impure waves flood his unconscious or subconscious mind. He cannot make them the object of his thoughts and fully conscious desire, with all the shocks and repercussions such a process entails. For a man and a Christian there is a law of integrity and personal purity, of self-respect, forbidding him to plunge so deeply into a world of sexual suggestions and tendencies. Here the "medical and psychotherapeutic interests of the patient" find a moral limit.

The moral struggle and psychical disorder

Original sin did not take away from man the possibility or the obligation of directing his own actions himself through his soul. It cannot be alleged that the psychic troubles and disorders which disturb the normal functionings of the psychic being represent what usually happens. The moral struggle to remain on the right path does not prove that it is impossible to follow that path, nor does it authorize any drawing back.

One should be slow. . . .

. . . One should be slow to lower man in the concrete, together with his personal character, to the level of the brute.

"Existential" man

The study of the constitution of real man ought, in fact, to take as object "existential man," such as he is, such as his natural dispositions, the influences of his *milieu*, education, his personal development, his intimate experiences and external events have made him. It is only man in the concrete that exists. And yet, the structure of this personal ego obeys in the smallest detail the ontological and metaphysical laws of human nature of which we have spoken above. They have formed it and thus should govern and judge it. The reason behind this is that "existential" man identifies himself in his inmost structure with "essential" man.

"Personalist ethics"

. . . it would be erroneous to establish for real life norms which would deviate from natural and Christian morality, and which, for want of a better word, could be called "personalist ethics." The latter would without doubt receive a certain "orientation" from the former, but this would not admit of any strict obligation. The law of the structure of man in the concrete is not to be invented but applied.

Social aspect of the psychic

What we have said up to now concerns man in his personal life. The psychical includes also his relations with the exterior world, and a praiseworthy task, a field open to your researches, is found in the study of the psychic in its social aspects, in itself and in its roots, and to make it serviceable for the purposes of clinical psychology and of psychotherapy. But one should take good care in this to make a scrupulous distinction between the facts in themselves and their interpretation.

Love of self

From certain psychological explanations, the thesis is formulated that the unconditioned extroversion of the ego constitutes the fundamental law of congenital altruism and of its dynamic tendencies. This is a logical, psychological and ethical error. There exists in fact a defense, an esteem, a love and a service of one's personal self which is not only justified but demanded by psychology and morality. It is a natural evidence and a lesson of the Christian Faith . . . Our Lord taught "Thou shalt love thy neighbor as thyself" (Mark, xii, 31). Christ, then, proposes as the rule of love of neighbor charity toward oneself, not the contrary.

An Apostolic Benediction

. . . be assured that the Church follows your research and your medical practice with her warm interest and her best wishes. You labor on a terrain that is very difficult. But your activity is capable of achieving precious results for medicine, for the knowledge of the soul in general, for the religious dispositions of man and for their development.

May Providence and divine grace enlighten your path! In pledge thereof we impart to you with paternal benevolence Our Apostolic Benediction.

[XIV]

Modern Education

"THE CHRISTIAN IDEAL of education" the Pope informs us "is identified with the latest findings of psycho-pedagogical science." But this ideal brings to psycho-pedagogical science a perfecting light, while "facilitating the educative process with the complete and fruitful development of the individual personality."

The Pope has stated a number of times that Christian education must never lose sight of the specific environment and background of individuals, and must, moreover, remain alert to the advances of the sciences and technology. And from his messages we gain a magnificent view of the content of a Christian education in the framework of the modern world. Ordered to a love of God and "the immutable truths and values which admit of no change in the heart and mind of man," the "new youth must breathe catholicity"; they must "feel the spell of universal charity"; they must have "a knowledge of their own personality, and thus also of the greater treasures of freedom"; they must be trained "to sound criticism" and imbued "with a sense of Christian humility"; their minds must "be directed to a more effective sense of justice"; the "innate tendency to regard themselves as a privileged caste and shunning the life of labor" should be eradicated; and they should be taught that the citizen should not stand "apart from the life led in his own country today."

R. C. P.

Education and modern methods

Certainly, great progress has been made in experimental psychology and in pedagogical methods. Men have sought, and not without happy results, to measure the importance of the different elements that condition the assimilation of scholastic material by means of the memory and the intelligence of the pupil. They consider material factors, such as furniture, lighting, types of books, composition of pictures and of sounds. And they consider intellectual conditions properly so-called, such as centering of varied interests according to local circumstances and age, and associations of memory which a well-adapted education fosters. It would be inexcusable for a modern teacher not to keep himself sufficiently informed of the work that is being done in this field. . . .

The Christian ideal of education

. . . the Christian ideal of education is identified with the latest findings of psycho-pedagogical science, surrounding it with a light which perfects it and facilitating the educative process with the complete and fruitful development of the individual personality. . . .

Man in his total reality

. . . Of essential importance [in adult education] is the inculcation of the art of distinguishing the true from the false, of awakening an appreciation of political and economic realities in conformity with the Christian concept of life, which, rejecting equally materialism and egotistic individualism, considers man in his total reality, composed at the same time of body and soul, an individual person and member of society, a citizen of this earth and one chosen for heaven. Only one with this composite outlook can provide a right interpretation of particular problems. . . .

The good teacher

Good teachers . . . should have perfect human formation, intellectual and moral. For the teaching office is a lofty position which calls for intellectual discernment and for goodness of heart, for a capacity for intuition and delicacy of spirit, for adaptability and adjustment as well as human depth, capable of bearing all for love of neighbor. Good teachers need a professional competency which should be at least above average, and better yet, outstanding on all levels of instruction and in each of the specialized fields, if it is not to be unworthy of a mission which serves not merely the people and the State, but also God, the Church and souls.

An exaggerated importance

. . . To the exaggerated importance that is accorded today to whatever is purely technical and material, reply with an education which always gives first place to spiritual and moral values; both to the natural and, above all, to the supernatural ones. . . .

Education rather than mere instruction

Good teachers . . . are careful to educate rather than merely to instruct; capable, above all, of forming and of moulding souls chiefly through contact with their own. . . .

A live personal expression

. . . Moral teachings bloom only superficially in the spirit if they are not accompanied by acts. Even the teaching of the merely scholastic subjects is not fully assimilated by the pupil if it does not flow from the lips of the teacher as a live personal expression; neither Latin, nor Greek, nor history, and much less philosophy will be accepted by the student with real advantage, if they are presented not with enthusiasm but rather as something apart from the life and person who teaches.

Christian education participates. . . .

. . . He [the Christian educator], like the grace of God, of which he wants to be nothing more than the helper, corrects and elevates at one and the same time. . . . In this way, Christian education participates in the mystery of the Redemption and effectively works with it. . . .

The fruits of a deeper Christian life

The first consequence for you [the teacher] of the deepening of your Christian life will naturally be a more elevated notion of your educational mission and a greater professional consciousness. We mean a more ardent will to achieve the greatest possible competency in your own field in anything pertaining to either theory or practice.

Society and the teacher

. . . A society that is really interested in intellectual and moral values, a society that does not want to slip and slide toward that materialism to which it is being drawn by the weight of the ever more mechanical life of technical civilization, must show the esteem that it has for the profession of the teacher, assuring him a return which corresponds to his social position. . . .

What is at stake in the school

The school cannot be compared to a chemical laboratory in which the risk of wasting materials, more or less expensive, is compensated by the probability of a discovery. What is at stake in the school is the salvation or ruin of every single soul. The innovations that can be judged opportune are those concerning the choice of means and secondary pedagogical directives, while the end and the substantial means will always be the same, just as the ultimate aim of education, its subject and its principal author are always the same, Our Lord and God.

Granted these principles, look then with a sure eye to the times and the hour to learn of new needs and examine new remedies. Confidently fix your gaze on the future which you will fashion with your own hands in the soul of your pupils. See to it that it be Christian and permeated with an ever increasing sense of justice, inspired by an ever wider charity and open to an ever deeper and more harmonious culture. . . .

No blind attachment to the past

. . . while exhorting you to remain faithful amidst the pressing needs of the present time to the rules that are the fruit of age-old conquests of human knowledge, We warn you against a blind attachment to the past which would today frustrate the efficacy of your work. If it is a good rule to treasure systems and methods proved by experience, it is also necessary to study carefully before accepting the theories and practices of modern schools of pedagogy. It does not always happen that the success achieved in some countries, different from your own, because of the character of the people and their different degrees of culture, will always guarantee that the same doctrines can be applied elsewhere without distinction.

Adaptation to the environment

. . . the work of education, since it must be carried on in a specific environment and for a specific background (*milieu*), must constantly adapt itself to the circumstances of this background and of this environment wherein this perfection has to be obtained and for which it is destined. . . .

In keeping with the Catholic idea

. . . This [a superior education by modern standards] is in keeping with the Catholic idea, which gratefully welcomes all that is naturally good, beautiful and true, because it is an image of Divine goodness, beauty and truth.

Keeping up-to-date

. . . Whether it be a matter of education, pedagogy, care of the sick, of artistic activity or something else, the Sister must have this feeling: my superior gives me a training which places me on a level of equality with my colleagues in the world. Give them also the possibility of keeping their professional capacities up-to-date. . . .

A broadening of views

It is time to broaden their [students'] views, beyond a world obstructed by factions, jealous one of the other, by extreme nationalism and desires of hegemony, because of which the present generation has suffered so much. Let the new youth be allowed to breathe Catholicity and feel the spell of universal charity that embraces all peoples in one Lord. Give them also a knowledge of their own personality and thus also of the greater treasures of freedom; train their minds to sound criticism, but at the same time imbue them with a sense of Christian humility, of just submission to the laws and the duty of mutual dependence among men.

Encourage them and tell them that Church and society expect great things of them and that there is much good to be done and that many noble undertakings await them.

Child of his own era

You, the teachers of today, who draw your sure directives from the past, what ideal of man must you prepare for the future? You will find that ideal fundamentally designed in the perfect Christian. By the perfect Christian we mean the Christian of today, child of his own era, knowing and cultivating all the advances made by science and technical skill; a citizen and not something apart from the life led in his own country today. The world will have nothing to regret if an ever-increasing number of these Christians is placed in all sectors of public and private life. It is largely for you, the teachers, to arrange for this beneficial introduction by directing the minds of your disciples to discover the inexhaustible strength of Christianity for the improvement and renewal of peoples. Then, spare no effort to awaken as soon as possible this moral conscience so that with the passing of the years the "honest man" will appear not as if by accident or as the final adventure of a life that has been often wrecked.

Form men of science and technology

Form men of science and technology on such foundations [as stated in the preceding quotation] and then it will not happen that they will strike the world with terror as happens today, when science has aroused, together with admiration, almost a fear of itself among peoples, and has caused formidable political, social and international problems; nemesis, perhaps, of the desired separation of science from religion. Some, at least, of the scientists themselves suffer from a lack of proportion, created by technology, between the material forces unduly developed and placed at the services of man and the pettiness and weakness in which their souls have remained. (Cf. H. Bergson, *Les deux sources de la morale et de la religion.*)

No privileged caste

[You, the teachers] Form strong men, capable of diffusing good all around them and of leading others with clarity of principles. Our times require that the minds of the pupils be directed to a more effective sense of justice, ridding them of that innate tendency to regard themselves as a privileged caste and shunning the life of labor. . . .

A painful experience

If it be your painful experience that the teaching Sister and the modern girl no longer understand each other well, this is not a thing peculiar to you. Other teachers, often parents themselves, are not in a very much better position. It is not using empty words to say that young people have changed, have become quite different perhaps. The chief reason for this difference in the young people of today may be that which forms the subject of the frequent lament: young people are irreverent toward many things that formerly from childhood were naturally regarded with the greatest respect. But young people of today are not solely to be blamed for their present attitude. In childhood, they have lived through horrible things and they have seen many ideals formerly held in high esteem break down miserably before their eyes. In this way they have become distrustful and aloof.

An old complaint

It must be remembered . . . that this complaint about lack of understanding [between teacher and pupil] is not something new. It is one made in every generation and it is mutual between maturity and youth, parents and children, teachers and pupils. Half a century ago and even a little before that, there was a good deal of sentimentality. People were fond of believing that they were "misunderstood" and said so. Today, the complaint, not devoid of a certain amount of pride, is more concerned with the intellect. The result of this misunderstanding is, on the one hand, a reaction which may sometimes exceed the limit of justice, a tendency to repudiate anything that is, or appears to be, new, an exaggerated suspicion of rebellion against any tradition. On the other hand, it is a lack of faith that shrinks from all authority and, spurning every competent judgment, seeks solutions and counsels with a sort of infatuation more ingenuous than reasoned.

A positive approach

Understanding young people certainly does not mean approving and admitting everything they maintain in their ideas, their tastes, their whims, their false enthusiasm. It consists fundamentally in finding out what is solid in them and accepting this trustfully without remorse or anger; in discovering the origin of their deviations and errors which are often nothing but the unhappy attempt to solve real and difficult problems; and, finally, in following closely the vicissitudes and conditions of the present time.

The heart of a child

. . . What deep and rich potentialities for love, goodness and devotion lie dormant in the heart of a child! . . .

"The art of arts, the science of sciences"

Maxima debetur puero reverentia—"We owe the utmost reverence to the child" (Juven. *Sat.* xiv:37) is a perennial invitation, as well as a warning, addressed to parent and teacher alike by the classic wisdom of pagan Rome, ages before the great pedagogue of the Christian Orient Saint Gregory Nazianzen reminds you both that the direction and formation of the young is "the art of arts, the science of sciences" . . .

The responsibility of the family

. . . Many families should not be allowed to believe they have satisfied their duties toward their children when they have sent them off to school, giving no thought to working hand in hand with the teachers, on whom they wrongly think they can completely unload a part of their own responsibilities. . . .

We encourage with all our hearts. . . .

. . . We encourage with all our hearts whatever will facilitate and render the cooperation of the school and the family ever closer.

The family chooses the teacher to prepare the adolescent to live his adult life in the state and in the Church, but it must not and cannot abdicate its directive office. Cooperation is natural and necessary, and in order to be fruitful, it presupposes a knowledge of each other, constant relations, unity of outlook, and successive adaptations. . . .

The scholar's task

Your task [the scholar's] . . . is to store the mind with knowledge, to examine knowledge acquired, to extend it, to advance the learning which is in your own particular sphere. In so doing you will take account of its contact and interplay with other branches of knowledge, and then, may we say, the shaping of our knowledge to meet the capacity and to gain the ready acceptance of men's minds. Thus it will be digested by them and what is of first importance, it will be nourishment and enlightenment to their spirit.

Bearing witness to the light

There is yet another motive which should urge you [scholars] to loyal and painstaking effort of tongue and pen. We mean the motive of dignity and reverence. For what is a scholar, a writer, a schoolmaster, a speaker, an educated man of whatever sort, if he be not in greater or less degree, in some way a man sent from God to bear witness of the light? (John i, 7-8). . . .

Age-old links

If the vicissitudes of the times have sometimes relaxed the age-old links between the Church and universities, the present-day disorientation of a mankind eager for unity and concord, and the spiritual anguish of so many persons of good will, all invite you to re-establish those links once again.

Mission of the university

In the first place, anybody who considers the university as a community of teachers and students dedicated to works of the spirit cannot deny that its mission is to be a center radiating intellectual life for the benefit of the national community, in that atmosphere of healthy freedom that is proper to all culture. . . .

The longing to participate

. . . if the university wishes to render fruitful for the new generations the centuries-old treasures which it has received in deposit, then it must bear in mind particular contemporary conditions.

For is this not a time, in effect, when in many countries large sectors of the population aspire to a participation in an authentic culture, when the economic and social difficulties of student and professional life pose grave problems for those in authority, and when, finally, modern means of information are incessantly increasing their influence, sometimes to the detriment of the real education of personal thought?

If we broaden our perspective, we notice that an analogous task confronts the great family of the universities, heir of mankind's cultural patrimony. In order to maintain themselves free of harmful particularizations, it is necessary to multiply the contacts between teachers and students of the various countries, to develop, by the study of languages and by useful collaboration, the appreciation of the intellectual riches proper to each; it is thus that people, far from becoming involved in competition and opposition to one another, will rather delight in supplying their reciprocal deficiencies.

Unity of truth

But this mission of the university [unity of truth], which brings together men and peoples in a peaceful intellectual collaboration, would be deceptive if it were not realized in a progressive coordination of the knowledge which they possess. Could the communion of minds be usefully achieved outside the unity of truth?

Specialization and synthesis

A university, as we observed a short time ago, does not mean merely the juxtaposition of abilities which are foreign to one another, but the synthesis of all the objects of knowledge. . . . And modern progress, with its specializations always more refined, renders this synthesis more necessary than ever before.

One danger

In truth, modern progress renders such a synthesis [of knowledge] more difficult and fragile as well, and the university must protect it from two contrasting dangers. The first would be the undue interference of the state, which, going beyond its powers, would presume to impose on education, for political or ideological ends, the specious unity of an arbitrary philosophy.

Another danger

. . . the university would fulfill its mission badly were it to abandon itself to pluralism or to a superficial syncretism; on the mere plane of natural knowledge, its task is to overcome the difference of subjects, to promote wisdom and to form the intellectual personality of the student. Let it be on its guard, therefore, lest it fail in its highest mission, namely, that of giving to young minds a respect for truth and of guiding them to independent lines of thought, indispensable to their intellectual maturity.

College of Europe

It is not without reason that the College of Europe has chosen for its headquarters a city rich in tradition and, We are happy to emphasize, a Christian tradition.[1] May the peace of its tranquil lakes be a symbol of the peace you [professors and students] are working to achieve by giving men today an awareness of their kinship to one another and by helping them to make the necessary sacrifices. May it be a symbol of the peace you are working for, thanks to a vocation that promises mankind still more priceless conquests.

May Our Lord deign to protect you, your families and your work for the common good.

---

[1] Bruges, Belgium.

[XV]

Modern Woman

IN A NUMBER of important messages, Pius XII has uttered the
most glowing words of praise for modern woman. Never, it
seems, "have events required on the part of woman so much
initiative and daring, so much sense of responsibility, so much
fidelity, moral strength, spirit of sacrifice and endurance of all kinds
of sufferings,—in a word, so much heroism . . ." The new world
situation and onrushing events have thrust women into spheres of
activity formerly monopolized by men, and, as a result, woman is
now "on a level with men in industry and labor, in the sciences and
in the arts, in the free professions and in public offices." And she
now stands on an equal footing with man in the matter of civil
rights. Hence, women are now required to play a larger and more
responsible part in the larger life of the community.

To the cry of fear that calls for the woman's active presence in
the home, the Pope responds that not only emancipation, but dire
necessities of life have taken women beyond the confines of the
home. While the Pope stresses the fundamental truth that the
home is still the center of woman's principal activity, he also calls
for a more conscious participation in political and social affairs,

especially on the part of women who are able to devote themselves more directly and entirely to them.

R. C. P.

Woman in the modern world

. . . The years of World War II and the postwar years have presented and continue to present to woman, in entire groups of nations, in practically all parts of the world, a tragic picture without precedent. Never, We believe, never in the course of the history of humanity, have events required on the part of woman so much initiative and daring, so much sense of responsibility, so much fidelity, moral strength, spirit of sacrifice and endurance of all kinds of sufferings,—in a word, so much heroism. . . . In the course of these awful years, women, old and young, have been forced to practice more than manly virtues, and to practice them to a degree required of men only in extraordinary circumstances.

The problem regarding woman

Let Us say at the outset that for Us the problem regarding woman, both in its entirety and in all its many details, resolves itself into preserving and augmenting that dignity which woman has had from God. For Us, accordingly, it is not a problem that is merely juridical or economic, educational or biological, political or demographic—it is rather one which, in spite of its complexity, hinges entirely on the question how to maintain and strengthen that dignity of woman, especially today, in circumstances in which Providence has placed us.

(172)

New duties

Catholic women and girls, formerly you would have thought only of worthily playing your sacred and fruitful role in the management of a wholesome, strong and radiant home; or you would have consecrated your life to the service of God in the composure of the cloister or in apostolic and charitable works. Beautiful ideals, where woman, in her proper place, and from her proper place, exercises quietly a powerful influence. But now you appear abroad, you enter the arena to take part in the battle: you have not sought to do so, but courageously you accept your new duties; not as resigned victims nor merely in a defensive spirit; you are determined to pass to the counter-attack and conquer.

What is at stake

The fate of the family, the fate of human relations are at stake. They are in your hands (*tua res agitur*). Every woman has then, mark it well, the obligation, the strict obligation in conscience, not to absent herself but to go into action in a manner and way suitable to the condition of each so as to hold back those currents which threaten the home, so as to oppose those doctrines which undermine its foundations, so as to prepare, organize and achieve its restoration.

To this powerful motive which impels a Catholic woman to enter upon a way that now is opened to her activity, there is added another, her dignity as a woman. She has to collaborate with man toward the good of the State in which she is of the same dignity as he. Each of the two sexes must take the part that belongs to it, according to its nature, special qualities, and physical, intellectual and moral aptitude. Both have the right and duty to cooperate toward the total good of society and of their country.

Emancipation, and necessities of life

Shall we conclude . . . that you Catholic women and girls must show yourself adverse to a movement which willy-nilly carried you with it into social and political life? Certainly not.

In the face of theories and practice which by different ways are tearing a woman from her mission, and, with a flattering promise of unbridled freedom, or, in reality, of hopeless misery, are depriving her of her personal dignity, her dignity as a woman, We have heard the cry of fear which calls for her active presence as far as possible in the home.

A woman is, in fact, kept out of the home not only by her so-called emancipation, but often, too, by the necessities of life, by the continuous anxiety about daily bread. It would be useless then to preach to her to return to the home while conditions prevail which constrain her to remain away from it. . . .

The plight of modern women

We see a woman who in order to augment her husband's earnings, betakes herself also to a factory, leaving her house abandoned during her absence. The house, untidy and small perhaps before, becomes even more miserable for lack of care. Members of the family work separately in four quarters of the city, and with different working hours. Scarcely ever do they find themselves together for dinner or rest after work—still less for prayer in common. What is left of family life? And what attraction can it offer to children?

An accomplished fact

Woman is the heart of the family; the care of the home, in which she is queen, constitutes the center and *palestra* of her prin-

cipal activity. But in this order of things, industry with its por-
tentous progress has brought an unprecedented transformation in
the history of human civic life. Industrial production, as you well
know, has drawn to it a considerable part of domestic labors, apper-
taining by nature to woman, and vice versa has obliged great multitudes of the feminine world to go out from the domestic hearth
and devote their day's work in factories, in offices and on planta-
tions. Not a few deplore such a change; but this is an accomplished fact, from which at present it is impossible to retreat.

Woman's role and public life

Your own role [women's] is, in general, to work toward making
woman always more conscious of her sacred rights, of her duties,
and of her power to help mold public opinion, through her daily
contacts, and to influence legislation and administration by the
proper use of her prerogatives as citizen. Such is your common
role. It does not mean that you are all to have political careers as
members of public assemblies. Most of you must continue to give
the greater part of your time and of your loving attention to the
care of your homes and families. We must not forget that the
making of a home in which all feel at ease and happy, and the
bringing up of children are very special contributions to the common welfare. So we rejoice in the fact, which you yourselves
rightly recorded, that among rural families, which are still such a
large part of society, woman's work in the home still goes hand in
hand with her contribution to the social and national economy.

Those among you who have more leisure and are suitably prepared, will take up the burden of public life and be, as it were,
your delegated representatives. Give them your confidence, understand their difficulties, the hard work and sacrifices their devotion
entails; give them your help and support.

Expansion of women's activity

Woman's activity is concerned, in great part, with the labors and occupations of domestic life which contribute to a greater and more beneficial extent than generally is thought to the true interests of social relations. But these interests also call for a group of women who can dispose of more time so as to devote themselves to them more directly and more entirely.

Fulfilling a duty

. . . in your social and political activity much depends on the legislation of the State and the administration of local bodies. Accordingly, the electoral ballot in the hands of Catholic women is an important means toward the fulfillment of their strict duty in conscience, especially at the present time. The State and politics have, in fact, precisely the office of securing for the family of every social class conditions necessary for them to exist and to evolve as economic, juridical, and moral units. Then the family will really be the vital nucleus of men who are earning honestly their temporal and eternal welfare.

Equality

In their personal dignity as children of God a man and woman are absolutely equal, as they are in relation to the last end of human life, which is everlasting union with God in the happiness of heaven. It is the undying glory of the Church that she put these truths in their proper light and honorable place and that she has freed woman from degrading, unnatural slavery.

Cooperation in civil rights

. . . Let us take the case of civil rights: These are at present the same for both, but with how much more discernment and efficacy will they be utilized if man and woman come to complement one another. The sensitiveness and fine feeling proper to woman, which might lead her to judge by her impressions and would thus involve the risk of impeding clarity and breadth of vision, serenity of judgment and forethought for remote consequences, are, on the contrary, of immense help when it is a question of throwing light on the needs, aspirations and dangers that touch domestic, public welfare or religious spheres.

Concrete action against war

. . . If indeed all women were to pass from that innate feeling which makes them abhor war to the concrete action to impede war, it would be impossible that the total of such imposing efforts, which bring into play those forces best calculated to move the will, that is, piety and love, it would be impossible, We say, that it should fail to attain its end.

The modern girl

The modern girl! You can measure better than many others the still unsolved problems and the grave dangers resulting from recent changes in the woman's world from her sudden introduction into all walks of public life. Was there ever such a time as the present when a girl has to be won and trained interiorly, according to her convictions and will, for Christ's cause and a virtuous life, remaining faithful to both despite all temptations and obstacles. . . ?

New conquests

. . . The Italian woman, and this is to her credit, did not make her entry into the public life of the nation with a light heart. Having attained her majority, independent and with equal rights, she is now on a level with men in industry and in labor, in the sciences and in the arts, in the free professions and in public offices. . . .

Christianity and the liberation of women

. . . When Christianity appeared on earth, pagan culture very often exalted women only for an ensemble of external and ephemeral endowments, or for their fineness of sensibility. This esthetic vision and this exquisite feeling reached, in fact, the highest and most delicate forms. The finely turned phrases in the immortal works of the poets of the Augustan age throb with feeling; the statues of the gods, divine creations of art, embellished the streets and forums, the temples and the courtyards of the sumptuous palaces. And yet all this was empty and superficial. Neither Athens nor Rome, beacons of civilization though they were, which spread so much natural light on family ties, succeeded by their lofty philosophical speculations or by the wisdom of their legislation in raising woman to the level which becomes her nature.

Christianity alone . . . while not failing to recognize those external and intimate qualities, was the first to discover and foster in woman those duties and callings which are the true foundation of her dignity and the motive for a more genuine exaltation. So that new types of womanhood come to light and make their influence felt under Christian civilization, such as those who were martyrs for religion, saints, apostles, virgins, promoters of wide-scale reforms, assuagers of all human sufferings, savers of lost souls, and educators. According as new social needs arose, their beneficent mission extended and the Christian woman became, as she is today, with every good reason, a no less necessary factor in civilization and progress than man.

[XVI]

Miscellaneous Subjects

IN THIS FINAL SECTION we cannot possibly avoid seeing what the other sections have already made manifest, that the Church can restore wholeness to our vision of things—a wholeness in which every legitimate human activity shows forth its splendor as the very embodiment of values which are as irradiations of the Divine. Thus, we owe to Pius XII a great debt for his marvelous and wholehearted exposition of a truth which the Incarnation impressed upon man, that spiritual life does not mean and cannot mean a contemptuous turning of one's back on things which are created manifestations of Divinity.

In a way calculated to stir the heart, Pius XII has taught us that spiritual life is essentially a yea-saying to all the wonderful things, material and spiritual, that have been poured out by God in the creative act, and to all that, which, while rooted in this act, comes forth only in the fullness of time, and to everything which man has produced in his glorious role as co-worker with God.

Evil becomes all the more repulsive when it is seen as a mutilation and disfigurement of a world whose norm is the goodness and loveliness that come from God. The truly spiritual attitude is therefore a redemptive one, in seeking to restore to human life its essential integrity and magnificence, and in making the whole environment shine forth with all the splendor that God wishes it to have. But this restoration takes place in and through the supernatural order, thereby elevating the world of man beyond the confines of nature, as great and sublime as it is. Hence, the true spiritual attitude, as a redemptive one, finds its inspiration and its strength in the Cross of Our Lord, since such an attitude is rooted in a self-abandoning love.

R. C. P.

The future belongs. . . .

. . . The future belongs to believers and not to sceptics and doubters. The future belongs to those who love, not to those who hate.

Where will the soul of man find peace?

The present hour is one of trial for the souls of men. In the dizzy whirl of material progress, amid the conquests of the human spirit over the secrets of nature and the forces of the land, the sea and the sky, in the fretful race to exceed the bounds reached by competitors in the field of enterprising research, amid the eagerness for profit and pleasure, in the strained efforts for a supreme power that is rather feared than desired, envied rather than attained, in the tumult of this whole modern life; where will the soul of man, which is naturally Christian, ever find peace? Will it be in mere self-complacency? Will it be in its vaunted mastery of the universe enveloped in the fog of illusion which confounds matter with spirit, the human with the divine, things that pass with things that endure? No, these delirious dreams will never set at rest the tumult of the soul and conscience of man, restless under the impulse of the mind which rises above matter, and which goes on, conscious of an immortal and unchangeable destiny, toward the infinite, toward aspirations which have no bounds. . . .

Enlightenment and decadence

The first and most serious stigma of our age is its knowledge, which renders inexcusable its outrage against Divine Law. Considering the degree of enlightenment and intellectual life—diffused as never before among various social classes—a marvel in which civilization takes pride, considering the keen and jealous sense of its own personal dignity and its inner freedom of spirit of which today's conscience boasts, the possibility or presumption of ignorance, concerning norms which govern relations between creatures and Creator should no longer find a place—nor, for that matter, the excuse founded upon this possibility which might lessen the guilt. This state of affairs, resulting in an almost universal moral decadence, has contaminated even spheres once traditionally immune, such as rural areas and the realm of tender childhood.

A collective responsibility

A great part of mankind, and let Us not shirk from saying it, not a few who call themselves Christians have to some extent their share in the collective responsibility for the growth of error and for the harm and the lack of moral fibre in the society of today.

Where shall we find men . . . ?

Where shall we find men deeply penetrated with the sense of responsibility for and close solidarity with the environment in which they live? . . .

Wonderful successes

If we consider the order of divine revelation and the mysteries of the Catholic faith, it is true that the immense progress that has been made in investigating and using the forces of nature, and still more the blare with which purely earthly culture is proclaimed, have so disquieted many minds that they are scarcely able to grasp supernatural truth. Yet the fact remains that zealous priests deeply imbued with the truths of faith and filled with the Spirit of God have had in our day greater and more wonderful successes than perhaps in any other age in winning souls to Christ. . . .

The living God

Today, after so many centuries which were centuries of civilization because they were centuries of religion, the need is not so much to reveal God for the first time as it is rather to recognize Him as Father, reverence Him as a Lawgiver, and fear Him as a Judge. If they would be saved, the nations must adore the Son, the loving Redeemer of mankind, and bow to the loving inspirations of the Spirit, the fruitful Sanctifier of souls.

This persuasion, taking its remote inspiration from science, is crowned by Faith which, being ever more deeply rooted in the consciousness of the people, will truly be able to assure basic progress for the march of civilization.

This is a vision of the whole, of the present as of the future, of matter as of the spirit, of time as of eternity, which, as it illuminates the mind, will spare to the men of today a long tempestuous night.

The Church and human reason

It is well known how highly the Church regards human reason, for it falls to reason to demonstrate with certainty the existence of God, personal and one, to prove beyond doubt from divine signs the very foundations of the Christian Faith; to express properly the law which the Creator has imprinted in the hearts of men; and finally to attain to some notion, indeed a very fruitful notion, of mysteries.

Understanding divine things

At all times, in the Catholic Church, human reason illumined by faith has striven as best it could toward a greater understanding of divine things. . . .

An exchange of views

. . . If it is true, as has been correctly said, that ideas, good or bad, guide the world, then one must realize the great importance of an exchange of views between philosophers who aim at projecting a ray of light on so many present-day questions—questions on which many of the most incompetent persons speak with such certainty and decision. . . .

The absence of public opinion

Public opinion is the mark of every normal society composed of men who, conscious of their personal and social conduct, are intimately concerned with the community to which they belong. When all is said and done, public opinion is everywhere the natural echo, the common resounding, more or less spontaneously, of events and the present situation in man's mind and judgment. Where public opinion fails to manifest itself, where it does not exist at all—whatever the reason for its silence or absence—one must see in this lack something vicious, a malady, a disease of social life.

A sham public opinion

We have . . . recognized public opinion as a natural echo, a more or less spontaneous common resounding of acts and circumstances in the mind and judgment of people who feel they are responsible beings, closely bound to the fate of their community. . . . What today is termed public opinion often exists merely in name, a name devoid of meaning, something like a vague rumor, a forced and superficial impression. It has nothing of that echo spontaneously awakened in the conscience of society and emanating from it.

Temptations

. . . The principal virtue of the journalist is, as always, an incorruptible love of truth. Yet how many temptations there are to make you depart from it: temptations bound up with the interests of a party and perhaps of the press itself on behalf of which you are working. How difficult it can be to resist them and to respect the limits beyond which the love of truth absolutely forbids anyone to go!—without forgetting, furthermore, that the "conspiracy of silence" can also offend gravely against truth and justice. Then there are temptations arising from public opinion, or more correctly from the opinions of the public, which the journalist cannot follow without reserve, being precisely the one who ought to bring them into line with the truth and with what is right, and so refine them and give them proper direction.

"The camera cannot lie," they say

When We have before Us a group of Newsreel executives, representing as you do the most influential agencies in that field of information, Our thoughts turn at once to reflect on the immense strides made by modern science in bringing to the entire world the important happenings of the day. It is not a matter of reporting scenes; the scenes are themselves presented as if taking place before the eyes. People in your own vast country see just what is being done on the other side of the globe.

Is that altogether true? so true that sound and safe judgments may be formed on the information given? "The camera cannot lie," they say. No; but it may be very selective in what it reproduces; and thus, truthful as it is, it may yet be turned into an effective instrument to create false impressions, and propagate the evil spirit of distrust, enmity and hate.

The lie

That which seems to us not only the greatest evil but the root of all evil is this: often the lie is substituted for the truth and is then used as an instrument of dispute. . . .

Insincerity

. . . Today it [insincerity] amounts practically to a system. It has been raised to the distinction of a strategy, in which the lie, the garbled word or fact, and trickery have come to be an accepted weapon of offense, which some people wield with the skill of professionals, boasting even of their competence. . . .

We do not propose to describe here in detail the havoc wrought by this tournament of "insincerity" in public life. But We are in duty bound to open the eyes of Catholics all over the world—and of all others besides who share our faith in Christ and a transcendent God—to the dangers which this prevalence of falsehood presents for the Church and Christian civilization, for the entire religious and even merely human heritage which has supplied the peoples of the world with the substance of their spiritual life and of their real greatness for the past 2,000 years.

When Herod of old was plotting anxiously to slay the Babe of Bethlehem he hid his plan under a pious mask, and tried his best to make the honest men into unwitting spies. Likewise today, his modern imitators move heaven and earth to conceal their real purpose from the masses, and make them the unconscious instruments of their designs.

Fear puts on the garb of Christian love

If there is something today that gives cause for fear, it is fear itself. There is no worse counselor, especially in the present conditions. It only brings dizziness and blindness and leads away from the right and secure path of trust and justice. . . .

Fear, which is a shameful thing in itself, excels in its many disguises. At times it puts on the misleading garb of a declared Christian love for the oppressed; as if suffering people could derive advantage from falsehood and injustice, from mob-tactics and from promises that can never be fulfilled.

Fear hides under the appearance of Christian prudence

At other times it [fear] hides under the appearance of Christian prudence and under this pretext remains silent when duty should require it to utter a fearless *"non-licet"* to the rich and powerful, and to caution them thus: it is not lawful for you, in following a greed for gain and dominion, to stray from the inflexible lines of Christian principles, which are the bases of political and social life and which the Church has repeatedly and with great clarity expounded to the men of our times. . . .

To stifle opinion

. . . To stifle the opinions of citizens, to reduce them forcibly to silence, is, in the eyes of every Christian, an outrage on the natural rights of man, a violation of the order of the world as established by God.

Justice and free discussion

Justice which is worthy of the name does not begin with prejudice and is not based on a decision previously taken, but gladly admits of free discussion and gives everyone due facility for thinking, believing and speaking. . . .

Justice is not an abstraction

Justice is not merely an abstract concept, an external ideal to which institutions must seek to conform as far as possible in a given historical moment. It is above all something inherent in man, in society, in its fundamental institutions, because of that sum total of practical principles which it dictates and imposes, of those more universal norms of conduct which form part of the objective human and civil order established by the perfect mind of the First Maker.

(187)

Blessed be those. . . .

Blessed be those who keep themselves and their peoples free from the bonds of preconceived opinions, from an influx of uncontrolled passions, inordinate egoism and an unjustifiable thirst for power.

Tolerance and freedom of conscience

. . . The ever-increasing contacts and indiscriminate mingling of various religious denominations within the same national groups have induced the civil courts to apply the principle of "tolerance" and "freedom of conscience." In such circumstances, let Us add, Catholics are in duty bound to practice political, civic and social tolerance with respect to the faithful of other denominations.

To promote a greater good

Reality shows that error and sin are in the world in great measure. God reprobates them, but He permits them to exist. Hence the affirmation that religious and moral error must always be impeded, when it is possible, because toleration of them is in itself immoral, is not valid *absolutely and unconditionally*.

Moreover, God has not given even to human authority such an absolute and universal command in matters of faith and morality. Such a command is unknown to the common convictions of mankind, to Christian conscience, to the sources of revelation and to the practice of the Church. . . .

The duty of repressing moral and religious error cannot therefore be an ultimate norm of action. It must be subordinate to *higher and more general* norms which *in some circumstances* permit, and even perhaps seem to indicate as the better policy toleration of error in order to promote *a greater good.*

Heartfelt gratitude

Nor can We pass over in silence the profound impression of heartfelt gratitude made on Us by the good wishes of those who, though not belonging to the visible body of the Catholic Church, have given noble and sincere expression to their appreciation of all that unites them to Us in love for the Person of Christ or in belief in God. We wish to express Our gratitude to them all. We entrust them one and all to the protection and to the guidance of the Lord and We assure them solemnly that one thought only fills Our mind: to imitate the example of the Good Shepherd in order to bring true happiness to all men: "that they may have life and may have it more abundantly." (St. John x, 10)

A window on the infinite

The function of all art lies in fact in breaking through the narrow and tortuous enclosure of the finite, in which man is immersed while living here below, and in providing a window on the infinite for his hungry soul.

Art—truth—grace

Souls ennobled, elevated and prepared by art—are thus better disposed to receive the religious truths and the grace of Jesus Christ. . . .

(189)

Interpreters of beauty and harmony

It is needless to explain to you [artists]—who feel it within your-self, often as a noble torment—one of the essential characteristics of art, which consists in a certain intrinsic "affinity" of art with religion, which in certain ways renders artists interpreters of the infinite perfections of God, and particularly of the beauty and harmony of God's creation.

Seek God here below

Seek God here below in nature and in man, and above all within yourselves. Do not vainly try to give the human without the divine, nor nature without its Creator. Harmonize instead the finite with the infinite, the temporal with the eternal, man with God, and thus you will give the truth of art and the true art.

The liturgy and the fine arts

And it is easy to understand how the progress of the fine arts, especially of architecture, painting and music, has not a little in-fluence in determining and forming the various exterior elements of the sacred liturgy.

No exclusively "human" or "natural" or "immanent"

... Whatever artistic beauty one may wish to grasp in the world, in nature and in man, in order to express it in sound, in color, or in plays for the masses, such beauty cannot prescind from God. Whatever exists is bound to Him by an essential relationship. Hence, there is not, neither in life nor in art—be it intended as an expression of the subject or as an interpretation of the object—the exclusively "human," the exclusively "natural" or "immanent."

The greater the clarity with which art mirrors the infinite, the divine, the greater will be its possibility for success in striving toward its ideal and true artistic accomplishment. . . .

Modern music and Catholic worship

It cannot be affirmed, however, that modern music and chant must be entirely excluded from Catholic worship. In fact, if these have nothing which sounds of the secular and is unbecoming to the sanctity of the place or to the liturgical actions, and if they do not spring from an inane desire for the novel and unusual, then it is certainly necessary to open to them the doors of our churches, as they can contribute in no small measure to the splendor of the sacred rites, to elevating the people's minds to higher things, and at the same time to the fostering of true devotion.

New forms and styles

What We have said about music may practically be said of the other arts, particularly of architecture, sculpture and painting. One cannot generally spurn and reject out of prejudice new forms and styles which are better adapted to the new material out of which they are fashioned. On the contrary if, with wise balance, one avoids excessive realism on the one hand and exaggerated "symbolism" on the other, and takes into consideration the needs of the Christian community rather than the peculiar judgment and personal taste of artists, it is altogether necessary to give a free hand to that contemporary art which, with due reverence and honor, serves the sacred places and sacred rites. Thus, it becomes possible for contemporary art also to join its voice to the admirable canticle of glory that the masters raised in past centuries to the Catholic faith. . . .

Tends it lovingly

. . . Stricken in succession by every scourge—floods, earthquakes, pestilential exhalations, devastating wars—the soil becomes in places a sterile, unhealthy desert, and now, serving as a hiding-place for deadly engines of destruction insidiously lying in wait for victims, is refusing to yield up its riches to man spontaneously. The earth is the chief wounded sufferer, the great invalid. Bending over it, not like a slave at his task, but like a doctor at the bedside of a patient, the cultivator tends it lovingly.

"O more than happy husbandmen"

. . . "O more than happy husbandmen" exclaimed the great poet of the country, "did they but know their blessings!" (Verg. *Georg.* ii, 458-459).

Mission of the dentist

Few people realize the dentist's mission. Dentistry requires an exact acquaintance with, and experience in, the sciences and arts. It demands tact, intuition and psychological finesse in order to acquire the art of persuasion and that moral authority necessary to anticipate and overcome those instinctive fears and hesitations on the part of the patient, more distracting than actual pain. You [dentists] need such patience, great physical resistance. You have to sustain a perpetual restraint on all your senses, your nerves are strained, your body, your mind, your will and your sensitiveness. Always standing, often in a constrained attitude, your eyes are strained, both hands are busy; they must be supple with the fingers contracted in the manipulation of several instruments at one time, every movement impeded by reflexes and reactions on the part of the patient, which are not always possible to perceive. And all this time you must remain imperturbable, calm, courteous, gentle, and full of charity.

The least defect of any of the tissues of the body such as the mucous membrane of the mouth may have repercussions on the rest of the health of the whole. The mouth expresses character and feeling which is not expressed by forehead and eyes only, but also by the lower part of the face; a single fold of the lip, almost imperceptible, often may transform and make an infinite alteration in the expression of the face. Thus there is a mysterious and surprising mission attaching to the treatment of the mouth.

A daily means of sanctification

Our deep pity for the vast world of invalids, along with the desire that professional activity may be for you [nurses] a daily means of sanctification, leads Us to exhort you to penetrate ever more deeply, and to make your own, the spirit of your excellent Association [of nurses and assistant health visitors]. Its lofty object is the elevation of your profession to the exercise of a true and sacred ministry. This obliges you to work, in so far as you are able, for the safeguarding in practice and in legislation, of the principles of natural and Christian right—principles which guarantee liberty and respect to the patient.

The model nurse

These two aims [safeguarding natural and Christian right], or if you will, these ideals inspiring your profession—if re-enforced and sustained by an ever progressing technical knowledge—will make each of you a model nurse. If you want to reach so high a goal more easily, take as your model the Divine Healer of all who resort to Him in the trials of sickness, the Master Jesus. Meditate frequently on the pages of the Gospel, which tell of the loving meetings of the Son of God with suffering humanity. With a pious glance, notice with what pity He bends over the suffering, with what feelings of fatherliness He gathers them to Himself and with what complete surrender He puts Himself at their service, at times traveling a long road to reach them. And do not fail to notice His supreme respect for their personality and liberty in the use of His miracle-working power in their favor. The fact that He usually waits for a request for a cure from the sufferer shows not only the intrinsic value of prayers, but also His respect for the human person and the human will. . . .

The ideal of the Christian nurse

To recognize Jesus in the invalid and to act yourself like Jesus with him—here is the ideal of every Christian nurse! In this way, it will come about that the image of Christ will be reproduced twice by every bed of pain: in the sick person, the Christ of Calvary expiating and resigned and in the one assisting, the compassionate Christ, divine doctor of souls and of bodies.

Sports in modern life

Your national scientific congress, dedicated to gymnastic and sports activity, answers without doubt to a necessity of the present time, opportunely detected by the sensibility of your conscience, which is well aware of what sport and gymnastics signify especially for modern people: of how diffused is their practice in all classes; of how lively an interest they arouse everywhere; and of the important and manifold effect that they have both upon the individual and upon society.

A joy not unlike that of the artist

What end do men pursue with so vast and diffused an activity [sports]? It is the use, the development, the control—by means of man and for the service of man—of the energies enclosed within the body; the joy which comes from this power and action, not unlike that which the artist experiences when he is using, and is master of, his instrument.

Crown of creation

... The King of the universe, in one manner or another, formed from the slime of the earth the marvellous work which is the human body, as a worthy crown of creation, and breathed in its face a breath of life which made of the body the habitation and the instrument of the soul, that is, raised the material to the immediate service of the spirit, and with that brought together and united in a synthesis, difficult of exploration by our minds, the spiritual and material worlds, not only by a purely exterior bond, but in the unity of human nature.

(195)

Thus, raised to the honor of being the dwelling place of the spirit, the human body was ready to receive the dignity of being the very temple of God, with even more superior prerogatives than those which are due to an edifice consecrated to Him. Indeed, according to the express word of the Apostle, the body belongs to the Lord, bodies are "members of Christ." "Do you not know," he exclaims, "that your members are the temple of the Holy Spirit, who is in you, whom you have from God, and that you are not your own. . . . Glorify God and bear Him in your body." (1 Cor. vi: 13, 15, 19, 20).

New force for an ancient code

From the same source of the Commandments is also derived force for the code, already known to the athletes of paganism, that genuine sportsmen properly observe the rules of games and competitions as inviolable and as so many points of honor, sincerity, loyalty, nobility of spirit, whereby they avoid the use of guile and deceit as they would the stain of dishonor; and the good name and honor of their adversary is of equal value to them as their own.

The physical strain thus becomes almost an exercise of human and Christian virtues: such, indeed, ought it to become and be, however great the effort required, in order that the exercise of sport may rise above itself and attain one of its moral objectives and be preserved from materialistic deviations which would debase its value and nobility.

From marvel to marvel

That which constitutes the human body, its structure and its form, its members and its functions, its instincts and its energies, is luminously taught by the most diverse sciences: anatomy, physiology, psychology and aesthetics, to mention only the most important. These sciences are everyday widened for us with new knowledge and lead us from marvel to marvel. They show us the stupendous structure of the body and the harmony of even its smallest parts, the inherent finality which manifests at the same time the rigidity of tendencies and the most extensive capacity for adaptation. They disclose to us centers of static energy alongside the dynamic impulse of motion and of impetus toward action. They reveal mechanisms, if they can be so called, of a fineness and sensitivity, but also of a potentiality and resistance, which are not met with in any of the most modern precision instruments. As regards aesthetics, artistic geniuses of all times, both in painting and sculpture, although they have succeeded superbly in approaching the model, have themselves recognized the inexpressible fascination of the beauty and vitality which nature has bestowed on the human body.

The religious and moral content of sport

. . . When the religious and moral content of sport is properly evaluated, one recognizes that this content should be inserted into man's life as an element of balance, of harmony and perfection, and as a powerful aid in the fulfillment of his other duties.

Helps and accessories

. . . By light of natural reason, and much more under the guidance of the Christian conscience, everybody can reach the sure norm that the training and the mastery exercised by the soul over the body, the joy experienced in the knowledge of one's strength and in one's success in sporting events, are neither the sole nor the principal element of human activity. They are helps and accessories, to be appreciated certainly; but they are not indispensable values of life nor absolute moral necessities. To elevate gymnastics, sport, rhythm, with all their associations, to the supreme scope of life would in truth be too little for man, whose primary greatness consists in much more elevated aspirations, tendencies and endowments.

Sports and gymnastics in the life of man

... Now, sport and gymnastics have, as their *immediate* end, the education, development and strengthening of the body from a static and dynamic standpoint; as their *more remote* end, the employment, by the soul, of the body so prepared for the development of the interior or exterior life of the person; as their even *more profound* end, that of contributing to its perfection; lastly, as the *supreme* end of man in general and common to every form of activity, that of bringing man closer to God.

Care of the body, yes—cult of the body, no

Sound doctrine teaches respect for the body, but not an esteem that is more than just. The maxim is this: care of the body, strengthening of the body, yes: cult of the body, divinization of the body, no, nor likewise divinization of the race, or the blood, or of their somatic presuppositions and constitutive elements. The body does not occupy the first place in man, neither the earthly and mortal body as it is now, nor the body glorified and spiritualized as it will be one day. The primacy in the human composition does not belong to the body taken from the earth's slime, but to the spirit, to the spiritual soul.

Sport on Sunday

... The Church does not forbid sport on Sunday. She looks upon it kindly, provided that Sunday remains the Lord's Day, the day for repose of body and soul.

How accept sickness and suffering ... ?

... The meaning of human destiny is not limited to the enjoyment or recovery of perishable health; it extends infinitely, even to the unspeakable realities of the other world. How accept sickness and suffering; how profit from them for the purifying of the heart and for esteeming more exactly human values: these are the problems which present themselves to every sick person, and whose solution he consciously or unconsciously seeks. ...

Physical defects

Numerous are the examples given us in present-day life, in addition to those spread throughout the course of history, which show that there is nothing to prevent a debilitated or impaired body from housing not only a sound soul, but at times a great one, even one touched by genius and heroism. Every man, although he be sick and therefore unable to participate in sport of any kind, is withal truly a man, who in his very physical defects is fulfilling a special and mysterious design of Almighty God. If he will embrace in the spirit of resignation this sorrowful mission, thus carrying out the divine Will and by the divine Will being in turn supported, he will be able more surely to travel life's way, which is for him a path strewn with stones and overgrown with thorns, among which not the least is the enforced renunciation of the joys of sport.

(199)

His special title to nobility and greatness of spirit will be to leave without envy to others the enjoyment of their physical prowess and of their bodily members and even to participate generously in their joy, as, on the other hand, sound and robust persons, in fraternal and Christian mutual exchange, should show and evidence to the sick an intimate understanding and candid benevolence.

Scouting and great Christians

The experience of thirty years has amply shown the formative value of scouting. How many great Christians, heroes and leaders, how many vocations to the religious life and the priesthood have been born within the troops. Fighting aberrations with zeal, you have constantly revised methods and recalled principles. . . .

The Scout Law

. . . Based on the foundation of the natural law, the Scout Law, by inducing endeavor, by the daily practice of voluntary good deeds, calls for the rectitude and loyalty young people so earnestly desire, and are happy to be helped in maintaining firmly. The Scout Law makes them detest deceit, falsehood and dissimulation. Feeling their strength grow, young people are generous by nature: they want to fight, stand up to difficulties: they feel the need of giving, of giving themselves, of going beyond themselves. In the open-air life and the quest of manual skills they find nourishment suited to their age. Favored by the morality of such an atmosphere, purity is assured and gives their energy a Christian reserve and delicacy.

Learning to live in modern society

From a tender age, the scouts' training must prepare, by concrete and suitable methods of observation and reflection, for the social, natural and supernatural realities. Scouts must learn to live in modern society. For this, they must be wisely instructed about its structure, its good points and its faults. Especially, they must prepare themselves to play an influential and responsible part, as far as they are able, in their *milieu* and in the parish community. The training of character, which is the object of scouting, must be directed toward social and apostolic work. It must train the scout to serve his neighbor, both in his personal contacts and also where those of temporal and religious institutions are concerned.

Love of nature

. . . If the scout loves nature, it is not as an egoist or a dilettante; nor does he enjoy merely space, pure air, silence, the beauty of the countryside. If he develops a taste for simplicity, for a healthy ruggedness in preference to the artificial life of the town and the slavery of mechanized civilization, it is not to escape the obligations of civil life. If he cultivates the best of friendships in a selected group, it is not to refuse contacts or neglect to render service. On the contrary, nothing could be further from his ideal. If he likes concrete realities, it is not that he despises ideas or books. He is careful to educate himself fully in so far as talent allows and necessity demands.

Tourism has a place

. . . From the beginning of the present century, the means of locomotion in the material order, the evolution of the world in the cultural order, have brought people closer together and almost abolished distances and have increased contacts among the most heterogeneous groups. Notwithstanding the diversified developments of travel and meetings, you [delegates to a tourism convention] have believed that there was still a place for tourism as such, and it is on this basis that, independently of particular conditions and aims, you have united and have assembled here.

While often the notion of tourism is reduced to that of a pleasure trip, you have avowedly taken it to mean something broader. And it is in this wider sense that We propose to address Our words to you, in order that thereby the value and effects of tourism may be better appreciated; a value, moreover, which is quite different according to the end that one wishes to attain and the manner in which it is achieved.

Among those who swallow up space. . . .

Among those who swallow up space, some, such as missioners and explorers, have been urged on by an irresistible desire for conquest: conquest of souls to make them heirs of the Kingdom of God; conquest of nations to extend this Kingdom to the ends of the earth. Is it necessary to recall the heroic journeys of St. Paul and of St. Francis Xavier, or those of Columbus, of Vasco da Gama, of Champlain, anxious to bring the benefits of Christian civilization to peoples not yet illumined by the light of the Gospel? Others, eager to make discoveries conducive to the progress of science or to the good of humanity, have gone to investigate the frozen territories of the polar regions (there comes to mind in this regard the great explorer and scientist of our age, Fridtjof Nansen), to attack unconquered peaks and forests, to break the silence of the deserts. And who is there who does not know of the peregrinations of Petrarch who, "not for any reasons of business . . . but moved only by a certain youthful ardor and by the desire of visiting,"

wandered through France and Germany, along the banks of the
Rhine and climbed Mount Ventoso, but always with his heart
turned toward Italy to which, from Mount Geneva, he sent that
tender and moving salute: "Hail, blessed land dear to God,
hail. . . ."

Common features of tourism

Since, then, there is such contrast among the variety of determining motives [of tourism], of aims pursued, of ways of travel,
of conditions of residence, of attitudes of mind, there must be
some common factor which is distinctive of tourism, and which
justifies your idea of representing here Christian tourism of every
kind.

Here then are the common features: to leave for a period,
whether long or short, one's habitation, daily occupation, one's own
relations, for the purpose of going away, exposing oneself at least
to a variety of unforeseen events, if not leaving things entirely
to chance; to submit oneself, joyfully or sorrowfully, to the greater
or lesser discomforts which are scarcely avoidable even in the best
organized touring; to come into contact with usages, traditions,
convictions or prejudices which are entirely foreign or even contrary to the ordinary mentality. Who is there who does not appreciate, though in very unequal measure, the advantages and the
discomforts which tourism entails?

"Tourist asceticism"

All these discomforts are in fact so many occasions for acquiring
and practicing what has been called "tourist asceticism." In fact,
they have the property of arousing a peculiar reaction which cannot be classified either as a sad and passive resignation, or yet as
the impatient rebellion of the senses and of the spirit. It gives to

the organism, temperament and character a healthy moral and physical resistance which, by enabling one to face with serenity the inconveniences and petty sufferings of touring, prepares a person to bear the future and inescapable trials of life with fortitude and courage.

The tourist becomes accustomed to the rigors or variations of temperature, to the uncertainties of a casual resting place, to excessive frugality, to the strange vagaries of cooking. His temperament is improved and becomes more docile as a result of his meeting with other characters not always likeable.

An important benefit

Another and more important benefit of tourism is that it refines the senses, enlarges the spirit and enriches experience. One sees, feels and observes. Many things in nature, in art, in regional customs or local traditions which, at first sight, may have seemed strange, not to say irritating or ridiculous, appear merely different and often indeed quite understandable, and at times very wise. Their value and interest are appreciated, and thus people come to be judged with ever greater justice and, in general, with greater forbearance and goodness, fruits of a better mutual understanding. In practice, tourism brings about a happy adjustment not only between individuals but also between nations, classes and parties. Not, indeed, that there should be any sacrifice of principle! The good is ever the good, evil is still evil, truth retains its rights as against error; but the habit is acquired of seeing what is good and true in others and of discerning the seeds of error in oneself.

Tourism elevates still higher. . . .

Tourism ordinarily elevates even still higher those who are able to engage in it properly. In nature, in the arts, in the usages of every clime, the observant tourist becomes accustomed to see in reflex—behind things, men, institutions—God, their Creator, their Father, their Supreme Legislator. He sees the course of world events and God's guiding hand. . . .

A seal impressed by the Creator

It is true that to the regard of the lawyer man does not always present himself in the more elevated aspects of his human nature, but often offers for study his meaner side, his evil inclinations, his wicked perversity, faults and crimes; nonetheless, even under a rational nature thus dimmed in glory, the true jurist should always see the human being, whose sins and crimes never erase the seal impressed upon him by the hand of the Creator.

Social assistance in the world of today

There is . . . a field of action in which the activity of the Conferences [St. Vincent de Paul Society] can make a direct contribution toward those objectives which We have frequently stated, namely, the field of social assistance. In this field you can render service while still adhering strictly to your institution, which, as you well know, intends to further every work that aims at promoting social justice and at improving the conditions of the poorer classes. Thus you must not consider as being outside your scope activities such as assistance to workers, schools for adult education, employment bureaus, provision of housing, summer camps for children, and other forms of social assistance which the youthful spirit of the Conferences will suggest to you.

Wonderful, indeed, is this universe. . . .

Wonderful, indeed, is this universe come from the omnipotent love of the Creator; wonderful are its elements which allow God's human creatures to mingle their voices in glorifying Him despite the apparent barriers of time and space.

Sources

In each section, the source data and other information are mentioned only with the first reference.

Key to Source Abbreviations

C.M. *The Catholic Mind*

Un.Ad. *The Unwearied Advocate* (3 vols.)

N.C.W.C. *National Catholic Welfare Conference*

Cath. Act'n *Catholic Action*

Am. Eccl. Rev. *American Ecclesiastical Review*

Nat'l Cath. Al. *National Catholic Almanac*

I.E.R. *Irish Ecclesiastical Record*

I. *Growth and Development*

The Church's vital law of continuous adaptation
    The Church—Foundation of Society
    F 20, '46. C.M. 44:193ff. Ap '46; Un.Ad., II:70ff.
    Allocution to College of Cardinals

The Church today and the Primitive Church
    Plea to Warring Nations
    My 13, '42. C.M. 40:1ff. Je 8, '42; Un.Ad., I:123ff.

No return to the past
    To the Catholics of Denmark
    My 24, '53. C.M. 51:504ff. **Ag** '53

Development of the Church
    Plea to Warring Nations

No retracing of steps
    Ibid.

The Church goes forward
    Ibid.

The Church is in time and space
On Faith and Marriage
O 6, '46. *C.M.* 45:129ff. Mr '47

The new needs of mankind
Encycl., "Summi Pontificatus"
O 20, '39. *C.M.* 37:890ff. N 8, '39; Paulist Press; *The Pope Speaks*, 148ff.

True progress
Christmas Address
D 24, '52. *C.M.* 51:111ff. F '53

Antiquity is no idol
Encycl., "Mediator Dei"
N 20, '47. *C.M.* 46:321ff. Je '48; Paulist Press

The meaning of tradition
On Tradition
Ja 19, '44. *Tablet* (Lond.) 183:54. Ja '44; *Un.Ad.,* I:182ff.

O blessed tranquillity. . . .
Christmas Message
D 24, '42. *C.M.* 41:45ff. Ja '43 (No. 961); *Un.Ad.,* I:144ff.

Eternal youth of the Church
Plea to Warring Nations

Across the centuries
Ibid.

Worthy of reverence and respect
Encycl., "Mediator Dei"

A living organism
Ibid.

The human side of sacred liturgy
Ibid.

Each period enriches the Church
The Sacraments
F 17, '45. *Am. Eccl. Rev.* 113:464ff. D '45; *Un.Ad.,* II:3ff.

Crisis of growth
Problems of Italian Workers
Je 29, '48. *C.M.* 46:609ff. O '48; *Un.Ad.,* II:215ff.

Address to members of workers' sector of Italian Catholic Action

Religious organizations and changing conditions
Apostleship of Prayer
O '28, '51. *C.M.* 50:501ff. Ag '52

Religious usages in a cultural frame
On Religious Vocations
S 15, '52. *C.M.* 51:379ff. Je '53
Address to 700 Mothers General and other Sisters attending the 1st Internat'l Congress of the Superiors General of Orders and Congregation of Women

The times in which we live. . . .
Concerning the Discipline to be observed with respect to the Eucharistic Fast, "Christus Dominus"
Ja 6, '53. *C.M.* 51:182ff. Mr '53

Continuity in the midst of change
Christmas Message
D 24, '42

Continuity of past, present and future
The Church—Foundation of Society

Contradictory aspects of historical evolution
The 5th Anniversary of Outbreak of War in Europe
S 1, '44. *C.M.* 42:577ff. O '44; *Un.Ad.,* I:202ff.

Different social structures
Church's Concern for Economic Life
Mr 11, '51. *C.M.* 49:706ff. O '51; *Un.Ad.,* III:121ff.

Never petrified
The Church—Foundation of Society

A progressive realization
Christmas Address
D 24, '51. *C.M.* 50:248ff. Ap '52; *Un.Ad.,* III:190ff.

II. The Complete Man

Christian humanitarianism
Encycl., "Summi Pontificatus"

Egotistical "isolationism"
Christian Message on the Christian Will to Peace
D 24, '48. C.M. 47:179ff. Mr '49;
Un.Ad., II:243ff.

The example of Our Lord
Christmas Message
D 24, '52. C.M. 51:111ff. F '53

Stronger than death
Encycl., "Summi Pontificatus"

A slothful tranquillity
Christmas Message
D 24, '42. C.M. 41:45ff. Ja '43
(No. 961); Un.Ad., I:144ff.

At the threshold of life
Divine Providence in Human Affairs
Je 29, '41. C.M. 39:1ff. Ag 8,
'41; Un.Ad., I:94ff.

Lesson of the Cross
Address to the sick
N 21, '49. Un.Ad., III:53ff.

Faith and limitless dimensions
The Spirit of Sickness
F 14, '54. The Pope Speaks,
I:28ff. First Quar. '54

The economy of salvation
Ibid.

Trust in God means. . . .
Divine Providence in Human Affairs

A glorious fusion
The 5th Anniversary of Outbreak
of War in Europe
S 1, '44. C.M. 42:577. O '44;
Un.Ad., I:202ff.

The Church liberates human energies
Encycl., "Summi Pontificatus"

Renewal of all human action
Address to University Graduates
Division of Italian Catholic Action
My 24, '53. C.M. 51:499ff. Ag
'53

The single measure of real progress
Labor's Dignity and Freedom
O 31, '48. C.M. 47:303ff. My
'49; Un.Ad., II:237ff.

The Christian religion and life here below
Encycl., "Sertum Laetitiae"
N 1, '39. The Pope Speaks, 198ff.;
Paulist Press

Obedience to God and human tranquillity
Easter Message of Peace
Ap 9, '39

Life is always a synthesis
In connection with the family days promoted by Italian Catholic Action
Mr 23, '52. Nat'l Cath. Al. (1953)
p. 70

III. *The Social Question*

Longing for a new world
The 5th Anniversary of Outbreak
of War in Europe
S 1, '44. C.M. 42:577ff. O '44;
Un.Ad., I:202ff.

A total transformation of society
To the Faithful of Rome

F 10, '52. C.M. 50:380ff. Je '52;
Un.Ad., III:201ff.

A social challenge
To Italian workers
Je 13, '43. C.M. 41:1ff. Jl '43;
Un.Ad., I:160ff.

A fatal error
Christmas Message
D 24, '42

The desire for gain versus human needs
The Life of the Farmer
N 15, '46. C.M. 48:442ff. Jl '50;
Un.Ad., II:117ff.

The degradation of man
Christian Principles of International Trade
Mr 7, '48. C.M. 46:421ff. Jl '48;
Un.Ad., II:197ff.
Address to Congress of International Exchange

Man is more important. . . .
Christmas Message
D 24, '52. C.M. 51:111ff. F '53

The violences of an egoistic economy
Challenge to Young Men
S 12, '48. C.M. 47:51ff. Ja '49;
Un.Ad., II:225ff.
Address to Italian Catholic Action and Catholic Action Representatives from 52 nations

Human values above quantitative considerations
Christmas Message
D 24, '52

The first and fundamental right
The Social Question in the New Order

Socialization
Future of Trade Unions
Mr 11, '45. C.M. 45:707ff. D '47;
Un.Ad., II:12ff.

State ownership and management
Address to 400 delegates to the 9th International Congress of the International Union of Catholic Employers
My 7, '49. C.M. 47:445ff. Jl '49;
Un.Ad., III:11ff.

Business and the national economy
Discourse to the Italian Catholic Association of Employers

The State and private property
5th Anniversary of Outbreak of War in Europe

A new basis for economic organization
Future of Trade Unions

An organic concept of society
Christmas Message
D 24, '42

Organic unity
World Federalism
Ap 6, '51. C.M. 49:393ff. Je '51;
Un.Ad., III:124ff.
Address to delegates of 4th Congress of World Movement for World Federal Government

Public authorities and coordination
On Wealth and Poverty

An integral economic policy
Ibid.

Workers and the national economy
Ibid.

Human society must remain human
Christmas Message
D 24, '52

The concept of the machine dominates
Ibid.

Technical progress and the general good
5th Anniversary of Outbreak of War in Europe

Tormenting the conscience
Christmas Message
D 24, '52

A spirit of cold calculation
Ibid.

Blindness to human dignity
Ibid.

A challenge to the American people
Encycl., "Sertum Laetitiae"
N 1, '39. *The Pope Speaks*, 198ff.
Paulist Press

IV. *The Modern State*

True concept of the state
The Modern State
Ag 5, '50. *C.M.* 49:460ff. Jl '51;
Un.Ad., III:92ff.
Address before 8th International
Congress of Administrative Sciences

A false common good
Ibid.

The State and the rights of the person
Letter to Harry S. Truman
Ag 26, '47. *C.M.* 51:633ff. O '53

The essential task
The Social Question in the New
Order
Je 1, '41. *Principles for Peace*,
719ff.; *Un.Ad.*, I:83ff.
Commemorating 50th anniversary
of Encycl. "Rerum Novarum" of
Leo XIII

The State and the common good
Encycl., "Summi Pontificatus"
O 20, '39. *C.M.* 37:890ff. N 8,
'39; Paulist Press; *The Pope
Speaks*, 148ff.

The goal of political and economic
activity
Christmas Message
D 24, '42. *C.M.* 41:45ff. Ja '43
(No. 961); *Un.Ad.*, I:144ff.

An organic and organizing unity
Christmas Message
D 24, '44. *C.M.* 43:65ff. F '45;
Un.Ad., I:221ff.

Totalitarianism, a mechanical unity
Judicial Jurisdiction of the Church

O 2, '45. *Un.Ad.*, II:44ff. (Italian
Text in *I.E.R.* 68:274ff. O '46)
Address to officials of the Sacred
Roman Rota

Authoritarianism versus true community
Ibid.

The "common good" of authoritarianism
Ibid.

"Authoritarianism" and the Church
Ibid.

Cooperation in the whole life of the
State
The Modern State

An expansion of rights
Encycl., "Summi Pontificatus"

Widening its field of activity
The Modern State

State planning
Ibid.

Sacrifices for the common good
To the Ambassador of Bolivia
Je 16, '39. *Principles for Peace*,
572ff.

Loss of respect for the common good
Christmas Message
D 24, '52. *C.M.* 51:111ff. F '53

The last word belongs to those. . . .
The Modern State

Blind worship of numbers
World Federalism
Ap 6, '51. *C.M.* 49:393ff. Je '51;
Un.Ad., III:124ff.
Address to delegates of 4th Congress of World Movement for
World Federal Government

The single individual today
Address to members of Pax Christi
S 20, '52. *C.M.* 51:564ff. S '53

Manipulation of the "masses"
Christmas Message
D 24, '44

Function of the juridical order
Christmas Message
D 24, '42. *C.M.* 41:45ff. Ja '43
(No. 961); *Un.Ad.* I:144ff.

Respect and obedience
Easter Message of Peace
Ap 9, '39. *The Pope Speaks*,
126ff; *Un.Ad.* I:4ff.

The normal man serves as rule
International Penal Law

O 3, '53. *C.M.* 52:107ff. F '54
Address to 6th International Congress of Penal Law

The law and human nature
Ibid.

Positive law
Ibid.

Security from arbitrary attack
Christmas Message
D 24, '42

The State and international community
Encycl., "Summi Pontificatus"

Enemy of true union
Ibid.

True meaning of sovereignty
The World Community
D 6, '53. *C.M.* 52:244ff. Ap '54;
America Press; *The Pope Speaks*,
1:64ff. First Quar. '54
Discourse to 5th annual congress
of the Union of Italian Catholic
Jurists

V. *Democracy*

The Incarnation and human dignity
Christmas Message
D 24, '44. *C.M.* 43:65ff. F '45;
Un.Ad., I:221ff.

The democratic form of government
Ibid.

The Church and democracy
Ibid.

Ideal liberty
Christmas Message
D 24, '53. *C.M.* 52:174ff. Mr '54

Two great rights
Christmas Message
D 24, '44

The people are awakening
Ibid.

Toward democracy
Ibid.

The call for democracy and better
democracy
Ibid.

"The people" and "the masses"
Ibid.

The curtailment of liberty
Christmas Message
D 24, '52. *C.M.* 51:111ff. F '53

Fundamental personal rights
Christmas Message
D 24, '42. *C.M.* 41:45ff. Ja '43
(No. 961); *Un.Ad.*, I:144ff.

Freedom
Address to new British Minister
Je 23, '51. *I.E.R.* 76:341ff. O '51

VI. *The World of Labor*

Dignity of working with matter
To Italian Workers
Je 13, '43. *C.M.* 41:1ff. Jl '43;
Un.Ad., I:160ff.

A necessary expression
Easter Message of Peace
Ap 9, '39. *The Pope Speaks,*
126ff.; *Un.Ad.*, I:4ff.

Human labor and divine creativity
Nobility of Work

Mr 27, '49. *C.M.* 47:564ff. S '49;
Un.Ad. III:6ff.

A humble workman
To Italian Workers

Transforming matter
Nobility of Work

The nobility of work
Ibid.

A parable for workers
Ibid.

VII. *International Community*

International unification advances
Catholics and International Life
Jl 23, '52. *C.M.* 51:563ff. S '53
A word of hope
Christmas Message
D 24, '42. *C.M.* 41:45ff. Ja '43
(No. 961); *Un.Ad.*, I:144ff.
A widening of horizons
Address to pupils and teachers of
the schools for adult education
in Italy
Mr 19, '53. *I.E.R.* 81:382ff. My
'54
A common aim
Christmas Message on the Christian Will to Peace
D 24, '48. *C.M.* 47:179ff. Mr '49;
Un.Ad., II:243ff.
The Church and universal community
The World Community
D 6, '53. America Press; *C.M.*
52:244ff. Ap '54; *The Pope
Speaks,* I:64ff. First Quar. '54
Discourse to 5th annual Congress
of Union of Italian Catholic
Jurists
Catholics are extraordinarily well
equipped. . . .
Catholics and International Life

Catholics and mutual understanding
Ibid.

Responsibility of Catholics
Ibid.

Faith in a higher community
The World Community

The community of mankind and the
natural law
Ibid.

An international order
Christmas Message
D 24, '41. *Principles for Peace,*
750ff.; *Un.Ad.*, I:110ff.

Order within and without
Christmas Message
D 24, '42

Democracy and the unity of mankind
Christmas Message
D 24, '44. *C.M.* 43:65ff.; F '45;
Un.Ad., I:221ff.

The universal good and the good of
each
Apostolate of Women
Address to the International Union
of Catholic Women's Leagues
Ap 14, '39. *Principles for Peace,*
561ff.; *Un.Ad.*, I:8ff.

Serving country and mankind
Address to the Foreign Press Assoc.
My 12, '53. *C.M.* 51:507ff. Ag
'53

The nations and world community
Encycl., "Summi Pontificatus"
O 20, '39. *C.M.* 37:890ff.; N 8,
'39; Paulist Press; *The Pope
Speaks*, 148ff.

The nations and international law
The World Community

No artificial uniformity
World Federalism
Ap 6, '51. *C.M.* 49:393ff. Je '51;
Un.Ad., III:124ff.
Address to delegates of 4th Con-
gress of World Movement for
World Federal Government

The unseen head
Christmas Message
D 24, '47. *C.M.* 46:68ff. F '48;
Un.Ad., II:187ff.

From Bethlehem to Golgotha
Ibid.

The discovery of brotherhood
To a group of newlyweds
Jl 10, '40. *Principles for Peace*,
679ff.

True brotherhood
Answer to Pres. Truman's letter
of Dec. 17, '49
D 20, '49. *C.M.* 51:639ff. O '53

The longing for larger groupings
Private Law and Its Coordination
Jl 15, '50. *C.M.* 48:754ff. D '50;
Un.Ad., III:90ff.
Address to a group of 200 priests
and university professors, in-
cluding representatives from 30
nations, assembled at Rome for
1st International Private Law
Congress

Away with barriers!
Christmas Address
D 23, '50. *C.M.* 49:201ff. Mr '51;
Un.Ad., III:109ff.

Prayers for the United Nations
Pray for Peace
S 2, '48. *C.M.* 46:675ff. N '48;
Un.Ad., II:221ff.
To American Pilgrims

Support for the agencies and offices
of the United Nations
Problems of Rural Life
Jl 2, '51. *C.M.* 49:708ff. O '51;
Un.Ad., III:140ff.

Public opinion
Address to Foreign Press Assoc.

VIII. *Cultural Diversity*

A guiding principle
Encycl., "Evangelii Praecones"
Je 2, '51. *C.M.* 49:574ff. S '51

Divine Wisdom
Encycl., "Summi Pontificatus"
O 20, '39. *C.M.* 37:890ff. O '39.
Paulist Press; *The Pope Speaks*,
148ff.

"Not anxious about diversities"
Christmas Message
D 24, '45. *C.M.* 44:65ff. F '46;
Un.Ad., II:59ff.

Gladly welcomes them
Apostolic letter to the bishops,
clergy and people of China
Ja 18, '52. *I.E.R.* 78:387ff. N. '52

A universal experience
The World Community
D 6, '53. America Press; *C.M.*
52:244ff. Ap '54; *The Pope
Speaks*, 1:64ff. First Quar. '54
Discourse to 5th annual congress
of the Union of Italian Cath-
olic Jurists

IX. *Peace*

Justice—a condition of peace
   To members of Pax Christi
   S 20, '52. *C.M.* 51:564ff. S '53

Peace, a moral and juridical process
   Christmas Message
   D 24, '43

To renew the face of the earth
   Encycl., "Summi Pontificatus"
   O 20, '39. *C.M.* 37:890ff. N 8,
   '39; Paulist Press; *The Pope
   Speaks*, 148ff.

A fervent wish
   Christmas Message
   D 24, '48

Confidence in the international community
   The World Community
   D 6, '53. America Press; *C.M.*
   52:244ff. Ap. '54; *The Pope
   Speaks*, I:64ff. First Quar. '54
   Discourse to 5th Annual Congress
   of Union of Italian Catholic
   Jurists

A fundamental postulate
   Christmas Message
   D 24, '39. *The Pope Speaks*,
   224ff.; *Un.Ad.*, I:40ff.

Mass psychosis
   To members of Pax Christi

X. *Science*

Traces of the Divine Intelligence
   Apostolic Brief; Archangel Gabriel,
   Patron of Telecommunications
   Ja 12, '51. *C.M.* 49:830ff. D '51

The conquests of science
   Mission of Professional People
   My 24, '53. *C.M.* 51:499ff. Ag
   '53
   Address to University Graduates'
   Division of Italian Catholic Action

Along new roads
   "The Admirable Conquest"
   F 8, '48. *N.Y. Times*, F 9, '48
   Address to Pontif. Academy of
   Science

Truth not opposed to truth
   Encycl., "Humani Generis"
   Ag 12, '50. *C.M.* 48:688ff. N '50

Our Masters
   At the Pontif. Academy of Science
   D 3, '39. *The Pope Speaks*, 221

A humiliating servitude
   Christmas Message

D 24, '43. *C.M.* 42:65ff. F '44;
   Un.Ad., I:172ff.

Man learns from two books. . . .
   At the Pontif. Academy of Science

Facts and their interpretation
   Address to delegates of 1st International Symposium of Medical
   Genetics
   S 7, '53. *Nat'l Cath. Al.* (1954)
   69ff.

No barriers to truth
   Ibid.

The act of knowing
   On Statistics
   S 10, '53. *C.M.* 52:58ff. Ja '54
   Address to International Institute
   of Statistics

The conquest of cosmic space
   Progress of Astronomy
   S 7, '52. *C.M.* 50:742ff. D '52
   Address to World Astronomical
   Congress

Mastering the immense universe
   Ibid.

A wonderful climb to the heavens
Ibid.

The deep interior of the solar orb
Ibid.

Bold and unafraid
Ibid.

The spirit of infinitesimal man
Ibid.

The meeting of spirit and Spirit
Ibid.

An unspeakable harmony
Modern Science and the Existence
of God
N 22, '51. America Press: *C.M.*
50:182ff. Mr '52; *Un.Ad.,*
III:174ff.
Address to Pontif. Academy of
Science

Illustrations in the midst of shadows
Ibid.

Philosophical arguments
Ibid.

Vestiges of God
Ibid.

The presence of God
Challenge to Young Men
S 12, '48. *C.M.* 47:51ff. Ja '49;
Un.Ad., II:225ff.
Address to Italian Catholic Action
and Catholic Action represen-
tatives from 52 nations

Inexhaustible riches
Address to a Congress on Radi-
ology
Ap 5, '54. *C.M.* 52:441ff. Jl '54

No reason to be fearful
Modern Science and Existence of
God

Mutability and the teleological order
Ibid.

The deepest recesses of nature
Ibid.

A vision of unity
Ibid.

Priceless services
Ibid.

"Everything is in flux"
Ibid.

The world bespeaks a Creator
Challenge to Young Men

The scientist of today. . . .
Modern Science and Existence of
God

Let there be light
Ibid.

Science's contribution
Ibid.

Science, philosophy and Revelation
Ibid.

Distinct from the world, but not
outside
Progress of Astronomy

The breath of goodness and love
Ibid.

Modern concepts and the Incarnation
Ibid.

An Apostolic Benediction
Ibid.

Genetics and eugenics
Address to delegates of 1st Inter-
national Symposium of Medical
Genetics

Noble and worthy aims
Ibid.

Philosophy cannot ignore genetics
Ibid.

The sciences of man
   On Statistics

Contribution of the science of statistics
   Ibid.

Statistics and truth
   Ibid.

Regarding the doctrine of evolution
   Encycl., "Humani Generis"

Nothing dearer. . . .
   Address to Staff of the École Française
   Mr 1, '48. *Angelic Shepherd*, pp. 262-3

Scientists and a new world order
   Address to delegates of Italian Society for Natural Sciences
   O 2, '42. *Principles for Peace,* 784

XI. *Technology*

Domination of the natural world
   Christmas Message
   D 24, '53. *C.M.* 52:174ff. Mr '54

A gift from God
   Christmas Message
   D 24, '41. *Principles for Peace,* 750ff.;
   Un.Ad., I:110ff.

Technology its own avenger
   Ibid.

Hateful abuses
   To Catholic Doctors
   S 29, '49. *C.M.* 48:250ff. Apr.
   '50; *Un.Ad.,* III:40ff.
   Address to 4th International Convention of Catholic Doctors

Technology can bring blessings
   Challenge to Young Men
   S 12, '48. *C.M.* 47:51ff. Ja '49;
   Un.Ad., II:225ff.
   Address to Italian Catholic Action and Catholic Action representatives from 52 nations

Gold, frankincense and myrrh
   Christmas Message
   D 24, '53

The people welcome technological progress
   Ibid.

The rudder has slipped
   Christmas Address
   D 24, '52. *C.M.* 51:111ff. F '53

A tormented age
   Encycl., "Summi Pontificatus"
   O 20, '39. *C.M.* 37:890ff. N 8,
   '39. Paulist Press; *The Pope Speaks,* 148ff.

The technical concept of society
   Christmas Message
   D 24, '52

The "technological spirit"
   Christmas Message
   D 24, '53

The "technological concept of life"
   Ibid.

A distorted vision
   Ibid.

"Progress in technology"
   Ibid.

The profound realities of organic life
   Ibid.

Restricting the free expansion of the intelligence
   Ibid.

"Admirable is the Divine Wisdom"
   Apostolic Brief; Archangel Gabriel, Patron of Telecommunications
   Ja 12, '51. *C.M.* 49:830ff. D '51

Radio, image of the Apostolic Faith
Encycl., "Sertum Laetitiae"
N 1, '39. Paulist Press. *The Pope Speaks*, 198ff.

Spanning the world
The Social Question in the New Order
Je 1, '41. *Principles for Peace*, 719ff.; *Un.Ad.*, I:83ff.
Commemorating 50th Anniversary of *Rerum Novarum* of Leo XIII

Thanks to modern technology. . . .
The Spirit of Sickness
F 14, '54. *The Pope Speaks*, I:28ff. First Quar. '54

Instrument of truth
Radio message to Catholics of Chile on occasion of Formal Inauguration of Radio Chilena
Ja 11, '54. *Ibid.*, I:16ff.

The good results are incalculable
Mission of Radio
My 5, '50. *C.M.* 48:575ff. S '50

Excerpts from address to 11th International Congress on High Frequency Broadcasting

St. Gabriel Archangel, Patron of Telecommunications
Apostolic Brief; Archangel Gabriel

For good and evil
Television: Its Public and Private Effects
Ja 1, '54. *The Pope Speaks*, 1:5ff. First Quar. '54
Letter to the Bishops of Italy

No one has the right. . . .
Ibid.

Possibilities of television
Ibid.

Thanks to God
Ibid.

Television and the family
Ibid.

The world in the home
Ibid.

XII. *Medicine*

A noble and sublime vocation
Moral Principles for Medical Profession
Ja 30, '45. *Un.Ad.*, II:1ff.

The progress of medicine
To Catholic Doctors
S 29, '49. *C.M.* 48:250ff. Ap '50; *Un.Ad.*, III:40ff.
Address to 4th International Convention of Catholic Doctors

The doctor who is worthy of his vocation
Ibid.

Zeal for humanity
Ibid.

The Catholic doctor
Ibid.

The ideal of his vocation
Ibid.

Precious creature
Moral Principles for Medical Profession

Spirit and dust: image of the infinite
Ibid.

Value of scientific knowledge
Moral Limits of Medical Research and Treatment
S 14, '52. *C.M.* 51:305ff. My '53; N. C. W. C. pamphlet
Address to 1st International Congress on Histopathology of Nervous System

Knowledge, a positive value
Med. Ethics and Law
O 19, '54. *C.M.* 52:46ff. Ja '54.
Address to the International Office
of Documentation for Military
Medicine

Science is not the supreme value
Moral Limits of Medical Research
and Treatment

Science is within an order of values
Ibid.

Two precious objects
The Surgeon's Noble Vocation
My 20, '48. *C.M.* 46:488ff. Ag
'48; *Un.Ad.*, II:207ff.
Address to 6th International Congress of Surgeons

Man is not the absolute owner of his
body

Moral Principles for Medical Profession

The bold spirit of research
Moral Limits of Medical Research
and Treatment

Natural and Christian morality. . . .
To Catholic Doctors

Exact scientific knowledge and morality
Moral Limits of Medical Research
and Treatment

Three guiding principles
Ibid.

Dangers and risks
Ibid.

Moral demands do not constitute a
brake
Ibid.

XIII. *Psychotherapy*

Recent psychological discoveries
Psychotherapy and Religion
Ap 13, '53. *C.M.* 51:428ff. Jl '53
Address to 5th International Congress of Psychotherapy and
Clinical Psychiatry

Conquest of mental illness
Nursing: a True and Sacred Ministry
O 2, '53. *The Pope Speaks*, I:54ff.
First Quar. '54
To participants in the National
Congress of Professional Nurses
and Assistant Health Visitors

The Church looks with satisfaction. . . .
Ibid.

The priest and the doctor
Psychotherapy and Religion

A healthy mind and religious development
Nursing: a True and Sacred Ministry

Man's charter
Psychotherapy and Religion

Basic points
Nursing: a True and Sacred Ministry

Tendency to the infinite
Psychotherapy and Religion

Misunderstandings
Ibid.

Primacy of the whole man
Ibid.

Psychic dynamisms and the soul
Ibid.

Real guilt and a morbid sense of guilt
  Ibid.

The pansexual method
  Moral Limits of Medical Research and Treatment
  S 14, '52. *C.M.* 51:305ff. My '53; N.C.W.C. pamphlet
  Address to 1st International Congress on the Histopathology of the Nervous System

A moral limit
  Ibid.

The moral struggle and psychical disorder
  Psychotherapy and Religion

One should be slow. . . .
  Ibid.

"Existential" man
  Ibid.

"Personalist ethics"
  Ibid.

Social aspects of the psychic
  Ibid.

Love of self
  Ibid.

An Apostolic Benediction
  Ibid.

XIV. *Modern Education*

Education and modern methods
  Aims of an Italian Teachers' Union
  Ja 4, '54. *The Pope Speaks*, I:11ff. First Quar. '54

The Christian ideal of education
  Education and the Modern Environment
  O 15, '48. *C.M.* 47:118ff. F '49
  Address to the Inter-Amer. Congress on Catholic Education at La Paz, Bolivia

Man in his total reality
  Address to pupils and teachers of schools for adult education
  Mr 19, '53. *I.E.R.* 81:382ff. My '54

The good teacher
  The Secret of Good Schools
  Ja 12, '54. *The Pope Speaks*, I:19ff. First Quar. '54
  Radio message to 5th Inter-Amer. Congress on Catholic Education at Havana

An exaggerated importance
  Education and the Modern Environment

Education rather than mere instruction
  The Secret of Good Schools

A live personal expression
  Religious, Moral and Intellectual Education of Youth
  S 4, '49. *C.M.* 48:569ff. S '50; *Un.Ad.*, III:31ff.

Christian education participates. . . .
  Aims of an Italian Teachers' Union

The fruits of a deeper Christian life
  Ibid.

Society and the teacher
  Ibid.

What is at stake in the school
  Religious, Moral and Intellectual Education of Youth

No blind attachment to the past
  Ibid.

XV. *Modern Woman*

Woman in the modern world
Papal Directions for the Woman of Today
S 11, '47. *Cath. Act'n* 30:17ff. Ja '48; *Un.Ad.*, II:167ff.
Address to Congress of International Union of Catholic Women's Leagues, Rome, Italy

The problem regarding woman
Woman's Duties in Social and Political Life
O 21, '45. *C.M.* 43:705ff. D '45; Paulist Press

New duties
Papal Directions for the Woman of Today

What is at stake
Woman's Duties in Social and Political Life

Emancipation, and necessities of life
Ibid.

The plight of modern women
Ibid.

An accomplished fact
To the Working Women of Italy
Ag 15, '45. *Un.Ad.*, II:35ff.

Woman's role and public life
Papal Directions for the Woman of Today

Expansion of women's activity
Woman's Duties in Social and Political Life

Fulfilling a duty
Ibid.

Equality
Ibid.

Cooperation in civil rights
Ibid.

Concrete action against war
The Cause of Peace
Ap 24, '52. *C.M.* 50:441ff. Jl '52
Address to delegates attending the 13th International Congress of World Union of Catholic Women's Organizations, rec'd in audience

The modern girl
On Educating Youth
S 15, '51. *C.M.* 50:376ff. Je '52; *Un.Ad.*, III:143ff.
Apostolic Exhortation to 1st International Congress of Teaching Sisters

New conquests
Woman's Apostolate
Jl 24, '49. *C.M.* 47:685ff. N '49; *Un.Ad.*, III:19ff.

Christianity and the liberation of women
The Cause of Peace

XVI. *Miscellaneous Subjects*

The future belongs. . . .
On the Problems and Dangers of Our Day
Je 2, '47. *C.M.* 45:449ff. Ag '47; *Un.Ad.*, II:150ff.
Address to College of Cardinals

Where will the soul of man find peace?
Our Common Catholic Interests
S 4, '40. *Cath. Act'n* 22:3ff. O '40; *Un.Ad.*, I:56ff.
Discourse to 9,000 representatives of Italian Catholic Action

To promote a greater good
The World Community
D 6, '53. C.M. 52:244ff. Ap '54;
America Press; *The Pope Speaks*,
I:64ff. First Quar. '54
Discourse to 5th annual congress
of Union of Italian Catholic
Jurists

Heartfelt gratitude
Encycl., "Summi Pontificatus"
O 20, '39. C.M. 37:890ff. N 8,
'39. Paulist Press; *The Pope
Speaks*, 148ff.

A window on the infinite
The Function of Art
Ap 8, '52. C.M. 50:697ff. N '52
Address to a group of Italian artists

Art—truth—grace
Ibid.

Interpreters of beauty and harmony
Ibid.

Seek God here below
Ibid.

The liturgy and the fine arts
Encycl., "Mediator Dei"

No exclusively "human" or "natural"
or "immanent"
The Function of Art

Modern music and Catholic worship
Encycl., "Mediator Dei"

New forms and styles
Ibid.

Tends it lovingly
The Life of the Farmer
N 15, '46. C.M. 48:442ff. Jl '50;
Un.Ad. II:117ff.

"O more than happy husbandmen"
Ibid.

Mission of the dentist
On Dental Practice
O 25, '46. C.M. 45:550ff. S '47

Address to the first Italian Congress of Stomatology

A daily means of sanctification
Nursing: a True and Sacred Min-
istry
O 2, '53. *The Pope Speaks*, I:54ff.
First Quar. '54

The model nurse
Ibid.

The ideal of the Christian nurse
Ibid.

Sports in modern life
Sports and Gymnastics
N 8, '52. C.M. 51:569ff. S '53
Discourse to Italian Congress on
Pedagogic and Hygienic Prob-
lems of Sports and Gymnastics

A joy not unlike that of the artist
Ibid.

Crown of creation
Ibid.

New force for an ancient code
Ibid.

From marvel to marvel
Ibid.

The religious and moral content of
sport
Ibid.

Helps and accessories
Ibid.

Sports and gymnastics in the life of
man
Ibid.

Care of the body, yes—cult of the
body, no
Ibid.

Sport on Sunday
To delegates at convention of In-
ternational Assoc. of Sport
Writers
N 10, '51. C.M. 51:254ff. Ap
'53

How accept sickness and suffering . . . ?
On Radiology
Ap 5, '54. *C.M.* 52:441ff. Jl '54

Physical defects
Sports and Gymnastics

Scouting and great Christians
The Values of Scouting
Je 7, '52. *C.M.* 51:255ff. Ap '53
Address to 7th International Congress of Catholic Scouting

The Scout Law
Ibid.

Learning to live in modern society
Ibid.

Love of nature
Ibid.

Tourism has a place
On Tourism
Mr 30, '52. *C.M.* 51:251ff. Ap
'53
Address to delegates to a tourism convention

Among those who swallow up space. . . .
Ibid.

Common features of tourism
Ibid.

"Tourist asceticism"
Ibid.

An important benefit
Ibid.

Tourism elevates still higher. . . .
Ibid.

A seal impressed by the Creator
The Nobility of Law
N 6, '49. *C.M.* 50:632ff. O '52
(see *C.M.* "Duties of Catholic Jurists" 48:53ff. Ja '50)

Social assistance in the world of today
Address to delegates of Italian National Congress of St. Vincent de Paul Society
Ap 27, '52. *C.M.* 50:693ff. N '52

Wonderful indeed is this universe. . . .
Radio message to Eucharistic Congress in St. Paul, Minn.
Je 29, '41. *C.M.* 39:11ff. Ag 8, '41; *Un.Ad.*, I:91ff.

A Selective Bibliography

I

Papal and Other Ecclesiastical Documents

Acta Apostolicae Sedis, Rome, 1909–.

Bishops' Statement on International Order (Nov. 16, 1944). National Catholic Welfare Conference. Washington, D.C., 1944.

Men and the Peace (Bishops' Statement, Nov. 17, 1946). National Catholic Welfare Conference. Washington, D.C., 1946.

Carlen, Sister M. Claudia, I.H.M.: *A Guide to the Encyclicals of the Roman Pontiffs from Leo XIII to the Present Day, 1878–1937*. H. W. Wilson. New York, 1939.

——: *Guide to the Documents of Pius XII* (1939–1949); with a foreword by Edward Cardinal Mooney. Newman Press. Westminster, Md., 1951.

Congar, Yves M.-J., O.P.: *The Catholic Church and the Race Question*. Columbia University Press. New York, 1954.

Gilson, Etienne: *The Church Speaks to the Modern World; the social teachings of Leo XIII;* ed., annotated and with an introduction. Doubleday. New York, 1954.

Huber, Raphael M., O.F.M. Conv., ed.: *Our Bishops Speak*. Bruce. Milwaukee, 1952.

Hughes, Philip: *The Popes' New Order*. Macmillan. New York, 1944.

Keenan, Charles, S.J., ed.: *Pope Pius XII on the World Community*. America Press. New York, 1954.

Koenig, Harry C., S.T.D.: *Principles for Peace: Selections from Papal Documents, Leo XIII to Pius XII;* with a preface by the Most Reverend Samuel A. Stritch. National Catholic Welfare Conference. Washington, D.C., 1945.

Millar, Raymond J., C.SS.R.: *Forty Years After: Pius XI and the Social Order*. Radio Replies Press. St. Paul, Minn., 1947.

Powers, Francis J., C.S.V., ed.: *Papal Pronouncements on the Political Order*. Newman Press. Westminster, Md., 1952.

Yzermans, Vincent A.: *All Things In Christ: Selected Encyclicals and Documents of St. Pius X*. Newman Press. Westminster, Md., 1954.

——: *The Unwearied Advocate; Public Address of Pope Pius XII*. 3 vols. The author, 25 Eighth Avenue So., St. Cloud, Minn., 1954.

Zizzamia, Alba: "Catholicism and Internationalism: A Papal Anthology," with a selective bibliography by Constantine Rackauskas. *Thought* (Fordham University), 28:485-527, Winter, '53-'54.

II

General Works

Burke, Thomas J. M., S.J., ed.: *Mary and Modern Man*. America Press. New York, 1954.

Carleton, Robert O.: "Modern history vs. God's plan." *Catholic World.* 176:276-281, Ja '53.

Connell, Francis J., C.SS.R.: *Morals in Politics and Professions*. Newman. Westminster, Md., 1946.

Conway, E. A., S.J.: "Catholics and Revision of the UN Charter," Part I. *America*. 88:230-232, N 29, '52; Part II. *Ibid.*, 89:129-131, My 2, '53.

Cronin, John F., S.S.: *Catholic Social Principles*. Bruce. Milwaukee, 1950.

D'Arcy, Martin C., S.J.: *The Nature of Belief*. Longmans, Green & Co. New York, 1931.

Einaudi, Mario and Goguel-Nyegaard, François: *Christian Democracy in Italy and France*. University of Notre Dame Press. Notre Dame, Ind., 1952.

Fitzpatrick, Joseph P., S.J.: "The Encyclicals and the United States." *Thought* (Fordham University), 29:391-402, Autumn, '54.

Gardiner, Harold C., S.J., ed.: *The Great Books; a Christian Appraisal*. 4 vols. Devin-Adair Co. New York, 1949–1953.

Graham, Aelred: *Catholicism and the World Today*. David McKay. New York, 1952.

Guardini, Romano: *Faith and Modern Man;* tr. Charlotte E. Forsyth. Pantheon Books. New York, 1952.

Gurian, Waldemar and M. A. Fitzsimons: *The Catholic Church and World Affairs*. University of Notre Dame Press. Notre Dame, Indiana, 1954.

Haas, Most Rev. Francis J., D.D.: *Man and Society*. Appleton-Century-Crofts, Inc. New York, 1952.

Halecki, Oskar: *Eugenio Pacelli, Pope of Peace;* in collaboration with James F. Murray, Jr. Farrar, Straus and Young. New York, 1951.

Higgins, George G.: "Religious Critics of the United Nations," *Catholic Mind.* 52:291-297. My '54.

Hildebrand, Dietrich von: *In Defence of Purity*. Sheed & Ward. New York, 1938.

——: *Transformation in Christ*. Longmans, Green & Co. New York, 1948.

Keenan, Charles, S.J., ed.: *Pope Pius XII on the World Community*. America Press. New York, 1954.

Koenig, Harry C., S.T.D.: "Pius XII and the United Nations." *Catholic Mind.* 52:143-148. Mr '54.

La Farge, John, S.J.: *Interracial Justice*. America Press. New York, 1937.

Lavanoux, Maurice: "Catholics and Religious Art." *Commonweal*, 59:34-36, O 16, '53.

Lubac, Henri de, S.J.: *Catholicism;* tr. L. C. Sheppard. Longmans, Green & Co. New York, 1950.

——: *The Drama of Atheistic Humanism;* tr. Edith M. Riley. Sheed & Ward. New York, 1950.

Maritain, Jacques: *Christianity and Democracy;* tr. D. C. Anson. Charles Scribner's Sons. New York, 1944.

——: *Ransoming the Time;* tr. H. L. Binsse. Charles Scribner's Sons. New York, 1941.

Masse, Benjamin L., S.J., ed.: *The Catholic Mind Through Fifty Years, 1903–1953.* America Press. New York, 1953.

Mersch, Emile, S.J.: *The Whole Christ.* Bruce. Milwaukee, 1938.

Moody, Joseph N., ed.: *Church and Society: Catholic Social and Political Thought and Movements, 1789–1950.* Arts, Inc. New York, 1953.

Mounier, Emmanuel: *Be Not Afraid;* tr. C. Rowland. Harper. New York, 1954.

Mouroux, Jean: *The Christian Experience.* Sheed & Ward. New York, 1954.

——: *The Meaning of Man;* tr. A. H. G. Downes. Sheed & Ward. New York, 1948.

O'Neill, James M.: *Catholicism and American Freedom.* Harper. New York, 1952.

Parsons, Wilfrid, S.J., E. A. Conway, S.J., and Thomas H. Mahony: *Peace in the Atomic Age.* Catholic Association for International Peace. Washington, D.C., 1947.

Pichon, Charles: *The Vatican and Its Role in World Affairs;* tr. Jean Misrahi. E. P. Dutton. New York, 1950.

Pollock, Robert C.: "Freedom and History." *Thought* (Fordham University), 27:400-420, Autumn, '52.

——: "History Is a Matrix." *Ibid.,* 26:205-218, Summer, '51.

——: "Luigi Sturzo; an anthology of his writings," with a Sturzo bibliography by John V. Walsh and Joan B. Quick. *Ibid.,* 28:165-208, Summer, '53.

Rankin, Charles: *The Pope Speaks: The Words of Pope Pius XII;* with a biography and a preface by the Most Reverend Edwin V. O'Hara. Harcourt, Brace & Co. New York, 1940.

Roberts, Archbishop, S.J.: *Black Popes: Authority, Its Use and Abuse.* Sheed & Ward. New York, 1954.

Scott, James Brown: *The Catholic Conception of International Law.* Georgetown University Press. Washington, D.C., 1934.

Sheerin, J. R.: "Pope Pius and World Federation." *Catholic World,* 174:241-245, Ja '52.

Schuster, George N.: *Cultural Cooperation and Peace.* Bruce. Milwaukee, 1952.

Stern, Karl: *The Pillar of Fire.* Harcourt, Brace & Co. New York, 1951.

Sturzo, Luigi: *Church and State.* Longmans, Green & Co. New York, 1939.

——: *The International Community and the Right of War.* Richard R. Smith. New York, 1930.

——: *Nationalism and Internationalism.* Roy Publishers. New York, 1946.

——: "Modern Conscience and the Right of War," *Hibbert J.,* 25:583-594, Jl '27.

——: "Modern Wars and Catholic Thought"; tr. J. P. Turley. *Review of Politics,* 3:155-187, Ap '41.

Suhard, Emmanuel Cardinal: *The Church Today.* Fides. Chicago, 1953.

United Nations, The: From 1945—An Appraisal; for 1955—Recommendations. The Catholic Association for International Peace. Washington, D.C., 1954.

Vanderveldt, James H., O.F.M., and Robert P. Odenwald, M.D.: *Psychiatry and Catholicism.* McGraw-Hill. New York, 1952.

Wright, Herbert: *Catholic Founders of Modern International Law*. Catholic University of America. Washington, D.C., 1934.

Yanitelli, Victor R., S.J.: "A Church-State Anthology; the Work of Father (John Courtney) Murray, S.J." *Thought* (Fordham University), 27:6-42, Spring, '52.